THE 3-TO-6 PM
BLUEPRINT

BUILDING SUCCESSFUL KIDS AND THRIVING COMMUNITIES

JonPaul Reed

The 3-to-6 PM Blueprint
Copyright © 2025 by Pure Momentum LLC.
All rights reserved.

All rights reserved. No part of this book may be used or reproduced in any manner whatsoever without written permission except in the case of brief quotations embodied in critical articles or reviews.

For information contact Puremomentum36@gmail.com

Written by JonPaul Reed
ISBN: 979-8-9941124-0-3

Table of Contents

Introduction: The Responsibility of Raising Tomorrow's Leaders 1

Chapter 1: The Battlefield: Why 3:00 to 6:00 is the New Frontline 5

Chapter 2: The 3:00 to 6:00 p.m. Gap: Our New Frontline ... 14

Chapter 3: The Sweet Spot: Focusing on the 8 to 12-Year-Old Mind 23

Chapter 4: Sports as the Vehicle, Not the Destination 33

Chapter 5: The Pure Momentum and Athlete University Model 41

Chapter 6: It's Not a Camp, It's a Sustainable Infrastructure.... 49

Chapter 7: The Daily Win: Measuring Short-Term ROI in Youth Development 59

Chapter 8: The Midterm Proof of Academic Improvement.... 70

Chapter 9: The Immeasurable Return: Cultivating Options, Not Just Athletes 83

Chapter 10: Funding the Mission: Tapping into Existing Family Resources 91

Chapter 11: Institutional Partnerships: Aligning with Schools and Districts 101

Chapter 12: The Logistical Solution: Implementing the Institutional Playbook Onsite 109

Chapter 13: The Parent-Athlete Dynamic: Nurturing Competition and Passion 119

Chapter 14: The In-House Playbook: Bringing the Micro Solution Home 130

Chapter 15: Mentoring the Child, Not Just the Jit 141

Dedication

This book is dedicated, first and foremost, to God—the source of all inspiration and the foundation upon which everything else is built.

It is also dedicated to my supportive family—my incredible wife, Renee, my daughter, Reign, and my son, Regal—who continually give me the space, time, and grace to pursue my passions and pour into others.

I would also like to extend a special thanks to Willie James Books for their support in making this writing journey seamless, structured, and stress-free.

Finally, this book is dedicated to Purpose—the driving force within us all. May every reader be inspired to seek, discover, and fulfill their own true purpose.

INTRODUCTION:
The Responsibility of Raising Tomorrow's Leaders

My name is JonPaul Nickolas Reed, and the entire goal of this book is to inform, inspire, and motivate a critical group of stakeholders: parents, guardians, educators, and city officials. The bottom line is that we have a tremendous responsibility as adults and caregivers of children. My fear is that when responsibilities are this big, people have a tendency to shy away from them. This book offers insight on practices that actually work in today's times, creating an option for a better way to do things.

Every community is different, but for the most part, we have to account for how life has changed in the last decade and adjust how we interact with children. The reality is, they are the next leaders; they're the ones we are turning everything over to. So, we have to create a system that allows us to motivate them to reach their potential—and that path is never a straight line.

What to Expect from This Book

I hope this book sheds some light on things that, for some readers, will be familiar and simply reaffirm their current practices. They'll read it and say, "Okay, I'm doing the right things." But for others, there will be points where they realize, "Okay, this is where I need to make an adjustment." It is my intention that this book is received in a manner that is not offensive or judging, but more like a practical guide that says, "Hey, these are the day and times of what we're doing, and these are things that we've put into practice that have real application and actually work." The ultimate goal is to offer a system where you don't have to rely on being an "expert."

The information in this book isn't just theory; it has been accumulated over the course of a lifetime—decades, in fact, four decades of life's work. It's not just based on my time running an after-school program or being a caregiver. I'm offering this up as food for thought and as a blueprint for success.

Empowerment, Hope, and Stronger Relationships

What I want readers to walk away with, above all else, is a sense of empowerment and hope. I know that every generation looks back on the next and feels like there's no hope for the future. The goal is to shatter that mindset and inspire true hope.

My deeper mission is to actually make the relationships between parents and kids better. At our center, one thing we emphasize is that we want to make the intimate time parents spend with their children more meaningful. The homework, the training, the back and forth—that's our job. Our job is to:

- Bring families closer: Make relationships stronger between moms, dads, husbands, and wives.
- Give officials a resource: Provide educators and city officials with a dependable entity—a blueprint—that is solely focused on developing and exposing children to meaningful and worthwhile experiences. While they handle the legislative and administrative side of their jobs, they can lean on this system.

Merging Five Key Perspectives

To create this stronger system, we have to address the large gap that often makes it hard for adults and children to find common ground. This book should be an opportunity for everyone to realize how difficult it is on both sides of the fence. This book merges five critical perspectives into a common platform:

1. The Child/Student: The perspective of the actual student, athlete, or child.
2. The Parent: The caregiver's perspective.
3. School Administration: The viewpoint of school administrators and officials.
4. The City/Municipality: The legislative and community perspective.
5. The Implementers: Our perspective as the people who are actually giving out the plan and the blueprint (e.g., Athlete University).

It's about making space and room for everybody to grow, because everyone—on all fronts—makes mistakes. It's about creating that fundamental level of respect.

The Power of Discipline as a Vehicle for Change

We also want to show people that disciplines can teach meaningful life lessons. When I talk about disciplines, I'm referring to the different activities where we choose to put our passion to create opportunity. At Athlete University, we call these vehicles. These vehicles—these disciplines—can inspire change and be the catalyst for the next leaders of tomorrow.

Ultimately, I want this book to showcase a group of people's life's work and inspire others who have a plan or an idea that they want to get out to the world. It's about encouraging people to find the proper platform and channel to get their message out. The biggest thing is showing the world that it is possible and that it is not as hard or far-fetched as you might think. As the saying goes, "A journey of a thousand miles starts with a single step." I want to encourage and inspire people to take that step today.

CHAPTER 1

The Battlefield: Why 3:00 to 6:00 is the New Frontline

My mission, which is the heart of **The 3:00 to 6:00 PM Solution: A Professional Framework for Building Success in Our Communities and Our Homes**, is rooted in a fundamental societal issue: if your parents couldn't, you didn't. This chapter is about establishing the "why" behind the framework—the **personal foundation** and **cultural context** that taught me the true meaning of the 3:00 to 6:00 PM window and compelled me to step onto the frontline.

If Your Parents Couldn't, You Didn't

Growing up in Jackson, Mississippi, was a journey, and if I had to put it into context, it was like living in an episode of **The Truman Show**. On the outside, it might have looked a certain way, but on the inside, the experience was totally different. Things that were completely normal to me—the everyday realities of our community—were often abnormal to others. This environment gave me a level of **desensitization** that worked both for and against me. It forged a unique ability to **focus, multitask**, and **compartmentalize**, making me tough and resilient. But it also came with flaws.

A huge takeaway for me, even at 40 years old, is that I have zero concept or concern for other people's perspective on me. I don't take it into account; I don't think, "What are people going to think about this?" This can be good and bad, but for me, it's primarily given me that **racehorse mentality**: put the blinders on and just run my own race.

Jackson was a vibe, as they say. We didn't know we were considered "country" or other stereotypes. I was blessed in whom I was born to—my mom is a unique, wonderful person. But outside of our immediate circle, I learned that the place I came from was essentially viewed as a **third-world country inside the United States**. I had no idea. Learning this truth shaped and molded me 100 percent.

Experiences That Shaped My Compass

My upbringing was rich with experiences that, in retrospect, served as a **compass**, constantly guiding my focus and sense of duty.

- **The Image of Emmett Till:** I was in second or third grade, about 7 or 8 years old, attending an all-Black Catholic school in a Title I empowerment zone. During Black History Month, we watched the documentary *Eyes on the Prize*. When the documentary showed the infamous picture of **Emmett Till**, whose mother insisted on an open

casket to show the world what had been done to her child, every kid in the room was shaken. It was an **image etched in my brain**, and I couldn't not look at it. It served as a visceral, lifelong reminder of what people are capable of, and it kept me anchored in understanding the injustices that have occurred.
- **The Baseball Field Confrontation:** As a young athlete, I played baseball, which was unique in African-American circles. During an All-Stars tournament, I was playing in an environment that was 80 percent white, and it was the first time I was ever called a **racial slur**. Though I had been told by other kids how to react in that situation, I initially didn't know how to feel. But when the kid said it again, I reacted instinctively. Suddenly, I was on top of him, and parents were pulling me off. They were yelling and screaming, wanting an explanation, but I didn't feel I owed them one. I just walked off. I felt like the adults should have policed the situation.
- **Losing a Friend:** In high school, my friends and I would cruise around town as a weekly ritual. One weekend, we were around three different places where shootings took place. We were just hanging out, but looking back, we should have had the common sense to realize when enough was enough. On the following Sunday, I decided to chill because it had been a crazy weekend and I had a baseball game the next day. I got a call later that night—my friend had been **killed, shot in the head during an attempted carjacking**

for his vehicle and rims. I couldn't get over it for a month and a half. It's a situation that happens way too much in a city of our size.
- **Witnessing Trauma:** When I was only 10, at a skating rink with my sister, an altercation led to a drive-by shooting. When the shots rang out my sister rushed us to the bathroom, and we had to wait until my mom came to get us. She kept telling me, "Don't look around, just look at me." But I looked to the left and saw **brain matter and fragments all over the wall**.

These situations didn't happen periodically, but they were regular enough to chip away at my **innocence**. They were the source of my desensitization, yet they also became the experiences that helped guide me.

Finding My Why: Duty Over Self

My upbringing serves as the foundation for the mission at hand—creating an **infrastructure to serve kids**. I was blessed. My mother was a registered nurse, and I was afforded experiences and opportunities that many of my friends were not. We were struggling when I was young, but I was unaware of it. However, I developed a strong sense of **duty**.

My friends couldn't share in many of my experiences. Yet, we were all the same, except for our parents. This realization led me to an undeniable truth: there are levels to experiences, and the only difference was the **economic, social, or resource-based abilities of our parents**.

I could have been born to a different set of parents. My experience could have been the total opposite. So, I kind of take the approach of I'm not special or unique, I'm just blessed.

Part of me **owes a debt back** to those people who didn't get those experiences. It's my purpose to aid people in reaching their potential through **programs, structure, discipline, and collaborations**. This is my debt to society, and as a father, it gives me a clear purpose to be aligned with the right things as I steward my own children. My overall purpose is wrapped up in an appreciation and understanding that it could have been totally different for me.

The Question is "Why Not?"

People often ask me, "Why do you do this?" I pose the question back: **"Why not?"**

- To whom much is given, much is expected. I have been given a lot.
- If those of us that know better, don't do better, how can we achieve more?
- The responsibility is already there.

I feel some people are just born with those **"mission papers."** Spiritually, or biblically, characters like Jesus, Solomon, and David all had a purpose. When we can discern our purpose, our **why becomes indistinguishable from our purpose**. My why is because I was blessed enough to know better, and I have the energy and understanding to act. I do because I can, I do because I should, and I do because someone has to. I will.

Nurturing Through Preparation: The Birth of Pure Momentum

My experiences, especially the absence of an active father, positioned me to go so hard as a dad and as a mentor. All of these elements created the work I do today: **Pure Momentum, LLC**. Our entity specializes and focuses on **development and exposure for student-athletes**. We are one part development, one part exposure, one part mentorship, and one part recruiting.

Our core framework is our year-round, Monday-through-Friday after-school program, which is the heart of **The 3:00 to 6:00 PM Solution**. This is the structure:

- **Pick-up:** We pick kids up from school.
- **Snack & Homework:** They come to our facility for a snack and homework time.
- **Discipline Rotation:** They then rotate into some kind of **structured discipline**.

Sports was always a part of my life, and it taught me everything: **structure, discipline, leadership, teamwork, conflict resolution, toughness, and grit**. Being able to facilitate and teach through sports makes learning easy because the experiences are real and daily. It teaches them that our society is about **competition**, but they shouldn't get caught up in the winning and losing; they should focus on the **process**.

My upbringing has blended with my purpose because I'm an athlete and a competitor, but I've changed my arena. The opponent is now those things that attempt to take away the future for people who haven't had the opportunity for exposure and motivation. My work is a **student-athlete resource center**, a platform that uses the vein of sports to justify the **energy, effort, hustle, passion, and focus** needed to secure your lot in life. We teach that you must hold yourself to your own standard and put your best foot forward every day.

Tying the Bow: Stepping In Where Parents Cannot

The chapter title, "**If your parents couldn't, you didn't,**" is the bow that ties all this together. Everything in my past was about what your parents could afford—the experiences. There were so many kids whose parents couldn't, so they didn't have these experiences: they couldn't travel, couldn't go to the mall, couldn't sit down at a restaurant.

I was often afforded opportunities, like being the only Black person among 40 or 50 people in a different state, simply because my mother could and chose to. This solidified the feeling that there must be other resources available.

- **Lack of Experiences Equals Lack of Knowledge:** Without certain experiences, kids lack the knowledge and information needed to be **well-rounded individuals** in society.
- **Why Kids Get in Trouble:** Often, kids act out in situations because they are overly excited or don't know how to behave. They don't know how to act in a restaurant because they've never been. They get overly excited on a trip because they've never traveled.

We have taken kids to the Kennedy Space Center and the WonderWorks museum, and one thing I realized is, how can these kids know how to act if they've never been in the environment? This kind of **socialization** is typically the parents' job.

Our entity is aimed at accumulating and using resources that already exist to **step in for those parents that cannot do**. We offer kids the opportunity to have experiences even when their parents' financial situation doesn't allow for it. We step in when needed to offer these experiences to deserving, underserved kids.

Final Thoughts: Purpose Over Approval

Sometimes we do things for the wrong reasons, chasing approval for someone else's gratification. But **purpose comes from solitude**; it is an internal component. I've learned to ask: What is that thing you would do if no one was watching, and would that thing be positive or negative?

The end result of your goal has to be **mission-oriented**; it cannot be selfish. I have learned to align my purpose with something that is pleasing to God, the source, and that serves society. This way, I don't have to worry about power or what I have to learn, because my mission is a self-fulfilling prophecy. Every day I go to work, I don't care if I only have one kid—I just know I'm doing what I'm meant to do.

As Steve Jobs said, you have to learn to listen to your heart and your intuition because it secretly knows what you want to do. We must **control the narrative** and not chase dogma, which is just the result of other people's thinking. This is what this framework is about: using past experiences to predict future behavior and dictate where we want to be.

CHAPTER 2

The 3:00 to 6:00 p.m. Gap: Our New Frontline

The biggest challenge facing our youth today isn't a lack of love from their parents; it's a lack of **structured, positive guidance** during the most vulnerable hours of the day. This is what I call the **3:00 p.m. to 6:00 p.m. Gap**, and understanding this window is the first step toward building a truly protective and proactive system for our children.

Defining the Gap

Let's look at this through the lens of the average working parent. They wake up and go to work—a 9:00 to 5:00 job that often stretches to 6:00 or 6:30 p.m. They love their child deeply and are concerned with their well-being, but they spend the majority of their time away from them. Even if they are physically present, they may not be engaging their child because they're simply working or exhausted. The people who love their child the most are not always able to pour into their child when they need it most.

Imagine the parent who gets the call at 4:30 p.m. that their child was caught doing something petty—grabbing a drink on the way home from school. This parent is immediately faced with a horrible dilemma: Is it more important to work and provide a financially supported life, or to be physically present to steer them and keep them from making bad decisions?

The 3:00 p.m. to 6:00 p.m. gap is that **unprotected period of time** when kids, especially those in the highly vulnerable 8- to 10-year-old range, are not being watched by people who are obligated to give them a certain amount of attention, love, and care. School is out, and they've been sitting down all day; they're tired and ready to let their hair down, so to speak. This is the time when they are most **vulnerable**, just like an adult after work grabbing a drink. That window is when **lack of discipline, lack of proper, guided authority, and a sudden rush of opportunity** can combine to create a negative outcome. We want children to have somewhere to be and something that they are being nurtured in to keep them from making choices motivated by simple idleness.

An idle mind is the devil's workshop.

I was once talking to a father whose middle-school-aged son, Jake, was at a pivotal age. The parents were separated, and the dad wanted structure, but the mom felt they shouldn't "force" the boy to attend our center. I told the dad plainly: "If you don't stick firm on this, the kid's going to find, for lack of a better term, a **do-nothing crew**, and they're going to do nothing together." The air went out of the room. I had to elaborate: If we don't give him something productive to do, his mind is going to attach to people who are doing things he thinks he should be doing. All of us—children and adults—need **guidance**, a path, and our steps ordered by people who have a sense of duty and responsibility.

The Battlefield and Its Impact

We call this three-hour window the **battlefield** because it is the time the kids are **most exposed, most uncovered**. They are out of school, they are in the streets—they are in the trenches. It is not me calling it the battlefield; it is the battlefield.

I can give you a clear, tragic example. I had a friend who, after school, would hang out with other kids at a local store. There was one boy who was constantly tormented and bullied. He wasn't a small kid, but he lacked the confidence of others, and his parents couldn't afford the designer clothes that often act as a form of protection in that environment. One day, during the 3:45 p.m. to 4:00 p.m. row session at the store—a routine cycle of emotional abuse—the kid who was being tormented was fed up. He had a small pocket knife. The aggressor finished his verbal assault and turned to walk away, satisfied with his performance, and that's when the victim lashed out and **stabbed him multiple times**.

In that moment, you had **two kids who were failed by the system**: one who had been emotionally beat down to a point where he had no armor left, and another who was physically harmed because of a lack of guidance during this critical time. This kind of danger is present everywhere in America. There's no one to step in and say, "Put the phones away. This time of day is going to be dedicated to building your personal skill set." It's like a bunch of **ticking time bombs**—kids hyped up on sugar and adrenaline, walking around with no structure. If you were in an environment with landmines, weapons, and no guidance, everyone would call it the battlefield.

Connecting the Gap to Key Outcomes

This time window directly connects to the foundational elements of a successful life:

- **Academic Outcomes:** As intelligent people have observed for centuries, **heredity and environment** make up a large portion of who we become. School is the environment for six hours, but the time immediately following is unguided. If kids use that time to "do what they want," they are not developing a personal skill set or working on a passion. They enter adulthood at 18 lacking essential mutual skills like **conflict resolution, focus, and being a team player**. They're less likely

to separate themselves from the crowd and secure opportunity.
- **Safety:** When children are not **policed**—meaning, not adequately checked and guided—they are allowed to influence the environment negatively. When adults without a personal duty to them are present, behavior goes unchecked. When adolescents aren't checked, they become violent, emotional bullies, or pushy because they are acting out from a place of lack. It's a cyclical effect of "your parents couldn't, so you didn't."
- **Mental Health:** The continuous exposure to an **unsafe mental environment**—like the kid who was bullied—creates so much paranoia and fear that their emotional capacity goes to zero. The mental harm manifests as a lack of ability to protect oneself, leading to an extreme, violent lashing out. Without the proper environment, academic outcomes, safety, and mental health are all directly affected by the lack of this 3:00 to 6:00 p.m. timeframe being **properly, assertively, and firmly policed**.

The Approach: Talking to Parents vs. City Leaders

The 3:00 to 6:00 p.m. gap is a concept with **macro and micro implications**. While parents and city leaders share the same space in society, their motives are different, and so must be the conversation.

For Parents (The Micro)

Parents are the superiors on this battlefield. They're the ones who train, but they can't always be on the field. The conversation must be framed around **direct personal impact**:

- **Self-Preservation:** An unruly, undisciplined child will cost you money and make your life harder. Their behavior will upset your ability to be in a state of peace and rest, crippling your ability to focus, grow, and continue your own goals and ambitions.
- **Preventive Mentality:** Your child needs a passion and a focus so that you can move away from an unfair, lopsided relationship where you are always disciplining them. A proper system **prevents problems before they start**, freeing you from the mental and emotional drain of constant petty issues.
- **Essential Need:** Your child needs a safe, healthy environment, and so do you. If a kid isn't focused on something positive, they will find something else to focus on, and that focus will have a direct reflection on your ability to earn, provide, and be an overall good steward to the child.

For City Leaders (The Macro)

City leaders have a more selfish interest at the core—they must be elected, and they are responsible for community alignment and safety. The conversation must focus on **efficiency and public order**:

- **Crime Prevention is Cheaper than Policing:** Crime rates, activity rates, and the general movement of society are used to measure the efficiency of city leadership. It is far easier to **prevent crime** than it is to stop it. By giving kids things to do during this window, we prevent them from getting "good" at motivated crime or identifying with negative elements.
- **Community Order:** There's an old adage in *Art of War* that says if you go to a city and animals are walking around in the street, it means the people responsible are not up to their responsibility. In our modern context, if the youth are walking around with no guidance, **the city is failing**. All adults started as children; if we don't police our youth now, we're guaranteeing higher crime rates and a more difficult-to-manage society later.
- **Delegation of Duty:** City officials can't be in every household. Their job is to partner with or allow people to come in who can do the job that they can't do for themselves. Investing in programs that fill the 3:00 to 6:00 p.m. Gap is a **high-leverage way to cut down on motivated crime** and steer children's energy into positive

places like sports, reading, skill-building, and goal identification.

The Reality of Inaction

Before I leave this discussion, I want everyone—parents and leaders—to live with the reality of their potential inaction.

I want to end with a brief narrative: A young boy, new to an area, was hanging out with friends after school. School was out, it was early evening. He saw a girl walking by and, wanting to look cool in front of his friends, he made a catcall, whistling and saying, "Hey, girl, you looking good." Everyone laughed it off, and they went their separate ways. Later that night, 20 adults showed up at his grandmother's door demanding he come outside. Sometime later, the boy went missing. His body was found—he had been murdered. That boy was **Emmett Till.**

I want everyone to ask themselves: **What time of day was it when he made that decision?**

It was during the **3:00 to 6:00 p.m. gap**. This tragedy happened decades ago, but the principle is timeless: If he had been in a center or a safe, structured place, none of that would have happened. We are losing children to just petty, superficial, immature things, whether the immaturity is on the child or the adult who reacts to it. We have to realize what's going to happen if you don't act—who are you allowing your children to move around with? Do you want your kid around people who would think like that, or people who understand that he is a child who needs protection? The moment is now to implement systems that protect our children.

CHAPTER 3

The Sweet Spot: Focusing on the 8 to 12-Year-Old Mind

When we look at children, we have a tendency to forget that **development happens in stages.** Understanding these stages is critical to making a lasting impact. Chapter 3 focuses on what I call "**The Sweet Spot**": the **8 to 12-year-old mind.** This period is a pivotal developmental phase where kids are actively coming up with their own ways of doing things, attempting to formulate their own opinions, and letting their unique personalities truly take shape. This distinguishes them from the 4 to 8-year-olds who are highly impressionable but not yet formulating complex opinions and ideas independently. By age 8, their own internal landscape is beginning to form, making them ready to receive focused guidance.

The Vulnerability of the Sweet Spot

The **8-to-12 age group** is the most directly connected to the outside world—the system—yet they possess the

least amount of experience in deciding what is good, what is bad, and what information they should take in. This is why **structure, discipline, and guidance** are absolutely paramount during this time. Studies suggest that a child's potential is largely set by the time they reach 9 years old (the third-grade benchmark). Our goal, therefore, is to give a focused trajectory to those kids in this 8-to-12 window who are still able to be reached. This work is two-fold; it depends not only on the child but also on the willingness and ability of the parents or guardians to receive help and allow mentors to step in.

It's easy to underestimate these kids. We don't realize how many decisions they are making on their own, how capable they are of navigating the system, or how adept they are at finding information. Think about it: how many times have you struggled with a phone or tablet, only for an 8- or 12-year-old to fix it in a second? They are the direct recipients of information in a digital world. It's our job to **target this demographic** and create programs and structure directly aimed at putting them in a position to be successful. They are the ones dealing with the information on a day-to-day basis, and they are the ones we must target to begin the revitalization of our communities.

Why We Call It "The Sweet Spot"

I call the 8-to-12 age group **"The Sweet Spot"** because, to put it plainly, they are the **low-hanging fruit**.

- They are the ones we have the most access to.
- They are the least protected and most vulnerable.
- They have the least amount of dedicated coverage or supervision.

A child between 4 and 8 is rarely left alone; they are always with someone. But at 8 years old, kids start moving around and making independent decisions. I guarantee there are more kids between the ages of 8 and 12 who are unsupervised than those between 4 and 8. This **massive pool of kids** is who we can access and influence in a positive way.

The Unique Mindset of the 8-to-12-Year-Old

What's unique about the way 8-to-12-year-olds think and make decisions can be understood by referencing the movie **Inception**. In the film, the goal was to implant an idea so skillfully that the subject believed it was their original thought.

The brilliance of this age group is that they take information given to them, and because they receive it without direct guidance or context, they believe these ideas are unique and new. They take foundational ideas from previous generations—whether it's slang, pop culture, or music—and evolve it into something new, which is what we call the new generation.

They have a unique ability to **repackage what was already there**. To the older generations, it looks new. But those of us who grew up in similar environments can easily identify where these new ideas originated. This leads to the classic generational disconnect where kids call you "old school" because they genuinely feel what they're doing is novel. Every generation goes through this phase of believing they have more knowledge or a better understanding than their elders. Because this is a natural order of things, we must **meet them at their level**, and strategically re-feed them information in a way that allows them to choose a discipline or a positive focus.

The Key Components of Effective Outreach

The most effective way to reach this group requires a **multi-faceted approach**, not a linear one.

1. The Right Timing: 3:00 to 6:00 PM

The best way to reach them is during the time frame when they are generally engaged in what many consider leisure: **3:00 to 6:00 PM**.

- After 3:00, they're out of school.
- If their parents aren't there, the average kid lacks the discipline to create their own structure.

This is a great opportunity to step in and engage them during a time they would normally be doing something non-constructive. This is where after-school programs that offer structure and discipline through sports, arts, or science are vital. This time slot is a no-brainer because it applies to all kids—from the **"latchkey kids"** with no structure to the highly-structured athletes. For the latter, it provides a crucial opportunity to hone and sharpen the skills or passions they're already working on.

2. The Right Variables

While the time frame is important, it's not the only piece of the puzzle. Effective outreach programs must also incorporate several other variables:

- **Relatability:** Most kids won't pay attention to things or people that don't pique their interest or seem cool. They need to connect with **mentors who are relatable**—people who have a shared background or who are business owners, athletes, or artists they respect.
- **Program Design:** The program can't be redundant or boring. Kids at this age should be experiencing many different disciplines to discover their interests.
- **Attention Span:** Programs must be designed to address and help **expand their attention span**. If a kid can only focus for 30 seconds to a minute, a unique, changing curriculum is necessary to keep them engaged long enough to develop a genuine interest.
- **Addressing Basic Needs:** We cannot be so far removed that we forget the small things. Sometimes the answer isn't a huge program; it's a simple act of care. Many of these kids are simply **hungry**.

I saw this just recently when a usually passionate, focused 8-year-old was struggling at an early morning baseball game. I quickly realized he was hungry. After getting him a simple breakfast burrito and a drink, the kid perked right up. Kids are very simple; we must ensure their most basic needs are met before we can expect focus.

Consistency and Impact: Case Studies in the Sweet Spot

We have a library of stories that demonstrate the power of consistent nurturing and early intervention.

Case Study 1: "Kenny" (Age 13, Entering the Sweet Spot)

"Kenny" came to us at age 13 as a talented multi-sport athlete who lacked discipline and structure. He was an incredibly big kid being raised by a single mom who was constantly battling him over trouble in school. Our goal was to create a relationship and bond where he felt safe enough to communicate.

One day, his mom called, furious after a bad day at school. She pulled up to the facility, all I heard was the screech of tires, and Kenny emerged, sobbing uncontrollably. The mom had reached her wit's end and had physically disciplined him. I had to mediate and explain to him: "Your mother attempted to tell you that what you were doing was wrong in a number of ways, and you did not respond. It is her job to make sure you get it, so she had to change her method of teaching."

That conversation, along with **consistent mentorship** through the ups and downs, became a turning point. We were a consistent presence he needed. Today, Kenny is doing incredibly well. He has already been offered scholarship offers from **FGCU Baseball, Arkansas State Football, and the University of Tampa Baseball**, and he has an outside chance of being drafted. His future is bright because he was willing to listen and take positive, consistent steps.

Case Study 2: "Chris" (Age 8, The Heart of the Sweet Spot)

"Chris" came to us at age 8 with significant behavioral issues at his charter school, including defiance, disrespect, and physical aggression toward teachers. In our facility, he was a model citizen because our energy is different—there is **immediate accountability**, and the facility has the "laws of the land" that must be respected. The disconnect was jarring.

I went to the school to talk to him, but the issues persisted for two months. I explained to him that the school system is based on paperwork, and all they're trying to do is build a paper trail to push him off. I tried to get him to understand that he needs to be a productive member of society, and that he can't draw negative attention to himself.

After a lot of back-and-forth, I suggested to his mom that the **environment needed to change**. I explained that sometimes there is too much bad blood between a teacher and a student, and some people can't turn over a new leaf. For kids, it is absolutely essential that you treat them with a **clean slate**. The mom requested a class transfer, and I am proud to say that since the move, Chris has had **no behavioral issues**. We had a direct impact on changing his trajectory by advocating for a fresh start.

I believe this highlights another essential component: as men, we must **show up**. We must pull up on these kids at their schools to hold them accountable. When a child sees you at their school, they can no longer pretend you don't care. We must protect the teachers and show the kids that we will not let them bully or step on others.

Empowering the Next Generation

Focusing on the 8-to-12 age group is about **prevention, not prescription**. It is the proactive tool we use to better our communities.

The Power of Unlimited Potential

First, we must understand what we are dealing with: a human being with **unlimited potential**. At this age, there is no cap on their ability. Society creates divisions, caps, and barriers, but these are really just figments of our imagination. We can influence, empower, and inspire them to understand that there are **no limits, no constraints, and nothing they cannot accomplish.**

If we allow them to pull from the prevailing notion that exists in society, they will adopt the idea that limits and barriers exist. The 8-to-12 bracket is the age group that most adults come into contact with the most—at malls, birthday parties, schools, playgrounds, and in sports. These are the ones who haven't been overly influenced, but they also have enough baseline knowledge to follow what we're saying. They might not grasp calculus, but they understand they need to count because they want money to buy something. They need **practical life application skills** to move and maneuver.

They are able to be taught and participate in the system, rather than having already accumulated so much trauma that they need specialized help just to defrag. This is the difference between an 8-to-12-year-old and some of the 13-to-18-year-old kids we deal with who are already carrying a heavy load of bad experiences.

Consistency is The Goal

Ultimately, **impact is the goal**—not money, fame, or clout. Impact is when a kid graduates and asks you to come to their ceremony, or when a parent reaches out and thanks you for being a consistent presence. You can't fake impact; the proof is always in the pudding. You must be there day in, day out. Our programs are designed to create that day-in, day-out dependability and trust, so when something goes wrong, you and the kid have a deep enough relationship that you can get the truth. This age group is our greatest opportunity to create that lasting, positive impact.

CHAPTER 4

Sports as the Vehicle, Not the Destination

The professional training we provide is built upon a holistic developmental model designed as a tested, scalable system for transformation. The true power of this system lies in its ability to take a child's natural interest—be it sports, music, art, or any other discipline—and use it not as the ultimate goal, but as a mechanism for imparting **critical life skills**. At Athlete University, we are fundamentally results-driven, and our model is centered on the actual development of a sturdy, adaptable skill set that an athlete or a child can use long after the final buzzer sounds.

We use the activity—the discipline, the sport—to teach and develop skill sets that will be beneficial to them as they matriculate through life. This approach is super unique because it allows for **real-world application** and the actual sharpening of these skills through daily **repetition**. While our kids certainly get a lot of "shots up," our model is workable for many different disciplines. It works for sports because skill building is tied into the very fabric of playing, but we can also use other areas to teach the exact same concepts.

The Core Concepts: Skill Sets for Life

What we are ultimately looking to teach are **foundational life skills**. Sports—or any intense discipline—provides the perfect microcosm for these lessons. The concepts we drive home on a daily basis include:

- **Conflict Resolution and Teamwork:** Understanding how to collaborate and solve problems within a group dynamic.
- **Hard Work and Determination:** Learning the value of effort and persistence.
- **Resilience:** The ability to move through disappointment quickly, processing failure not as an ending, but as a learning lesson—a life lesson.
- **Situational Awareness:** Understanding that there is a time and place for everything—a time for play, a time for structure, and a time for leisure work.
- **Emotional Management:** Learning to "turn the other cheek." We actively teach the child that our facility is not the place to "handle your business" with retaliation. Your business is now my business, and informing an authority figure is necessary for a non-chaotic, cohesive environment.

- **Respect for the Law of the Land:** You don't have to like everything or everyone, but you have to learn to coexist and respect the established rules and structure. For instance, you might not like the five-minute run when you first get here, but you have to sacrifice your preference to be a part of the environment.
- **Personal Responsibility and Safety:** We instill the rule that while you are with us, you belong to us. Running off without being properly checked out—even if you see a parent—is not acceptable. It's a safety non-negotiable that reinforces structure and accountability for everyone.
- **Toughness and Fortitude:** When you get bumped down, you have to be able to bounce back up and shake it off. We coach for a healthy level of intestinal fortitude. If you're truly hurt, we'll take a break, but we encourage resilience.
- **Leadership and Tolerance:** Sometimes, a child's skill level is higher than others. We encourage them to show tolerance and understanding, facilitating someone else's growth and development. We all have to coexist, and that requires figuring out resolutions when wants and needs collide.

Shaping the Framework: The 8-to-12-Year-Old Mind

These lessons are especially crucial for children between the ages of **8 and 12** because this is when they are formulating their core ideas. They are experimenting with new concepts and thinking these ideas are completely their own. I often reference the movie *Inception*: our job is to **plant the idea in their heads**, but we allow them to feel the confidence that they came up with it.

We need to **shape their framework**. Our approach is to give them **flexibility and freedom**—that essential sense of identity and creation—but always within a **clearly defined boundary**. We set the guidelines, and they are free to operate within the confines of those rules.

The moment they step outside the guidelines, the **structure, the discipline, and the organizational program structure steps in**. There is an already go-to, pre-designed response because we understand that these kids are constantly formulating and experimenting with ideas, many of which we are not even aware of. We allow for that sense of creation, but when the thinking is off or there's an imbalance, someone has to step in and reset those scales.

Navigating the Stakeholders: Coaches, Parents, and the Athlete

Balancing the mindset of results-focused coaches and financially-motivated parents who often see the activity solely as a path to scholarships, rather than a developmental tool for the whole person, is our unique contribution.

Our Role: The Navigator

Our role is to step back and place the **development of each individual child at the forefront**. This focus is what truly promotes sustainable skill building and a healthy understanding of teamwork. We keep a clear understanding of where we are at all times—we are the **navigator** in this vehicle, understanding the destination, the pit stops, and what is in between. We balance all the competing motivations.

The Coach's Role: The Team Focus

A coach's goal is typically for the team to perform at its highest degree, which is a noble pursuit. However, they are often **organizationally motivated and team-oriented**. For the team to succeed, the individuals must not only have the ability to execute skills but also have a willingness to see others do well. The coach's primary focus is winning.

The Parent's Role: The Mirror

Parents are often financially motivated and responsible for their child's well-being. They may focus on development, but they are not always well-versed in the discipline and often assume the coach is managing the individual development—which is often not the case.

Our focus with parents is encouraging them to be the **mirror**: the eyes and ears who reflect the program's foundation back to the child. We want the parent to avoid being the bad guy, instead asking insightful questions:

- "How did today go? What did you think? What did you experience?"
- "How could you have done this differently? Did you prepare?"
- "What was your routine?"

This reminds the child of the foundation the program has set and reinforces the long-term, skill-based perspective. These day-to-day wins and losses don't really mean much in the grand scheme; it's about the skills and scenarios they get a chance to go through.

Find the Passion: Creating an Internal Driving Force

It all starts with interest, likes, and dislikes. Our focus is to help the child identify a **passion or discipline** they are genuinely excited about. Without passion, they lack **internal driving force** and will only be guided by external motivation.

When a child is motivated on their own accord:

- **Discipline becomes easier** for the parent, who now has something the child loves that can be restricted without resorting to physical interaction.
- They become **better teammates** because they are taking an interest, practicing, and improving, which teaches them that **preparation precedes success**.

We must not negotiate non-negotiables. **Discipline is critical**. We will always hear the child out, but the rules are the rules. We don't waver, fluctuate, or backtrack because we know what is necessary for success, and we hold the kids to that standard. Even if the child isn't an "athlete," we still hold them to the same high standard because the common thread in American society is **competition**. We live in a capitalist society, which means we must learn how to compete for limited resources. Our duty is to teach them to compete with a healthy mindset and regard for both themselves and their competitors.

Experience is Key: Trying Different Things

As parents, we sometimes have a tendency to want to force a child into a lane. The reality is that the best fit is often more about **disposition** than it is about lineage. Heredity plays a role in ability, but if your kid is super social or, conversely, not super social, they might prefer a team or an individual sport, respectively.

Our goal should be on identifying the child's disposition so we can figure out what environment they will be comfortable in—the environment where they can give their best effort. If a non-physical child is forced into football, it's not a comfort zone.

We urge everyone to **try different things**. One of the great things about our program is that kids get a chance to experience everything: football, baseball, basketball, soccer, lacrosse, even cheering and dance, alongside activities like arts and crafts, painting, and designing.

In order to know what we like, we must first know what we don't like. You only know vanilla is your favorite ice cream because you tried chocolate and pistachio and realized you didn't like them. Our desires have a lot to do with our dislikes, but the only thing that teaches us that is **experience**. Our job is to aid that process and cut the learning curve down.

In the end, less is more. The sport is the **vehicle** because it is the apparatus taking the child from one thing to the next. The pressure to make it "our thing" as a parent takes the fun out of it. If you have questions for your child, ask them over ice cream or a fun activity, and interact with them as an equal—not as a bad investment. The outcome of any game is the outcome, but the reality is, the outcome is a **byproduct of the preparation** (or lack thereof). Our job is to ensure the standard of preparation is in place.

We are building **character traits and habits** that will follow them for life. The sport is not the destination; it is the tool. It is our job to teach children to use these things as tools, and to not let these things use them. **Keeping things in proper perspective is key**: no college coach is going to deny a scholarship opportunity because your child only scored five points in a 12-year-old league basketball game. Our focus is on creating **good habits**.

CHAPTER 5

The Pure Momentum and Athlete University Model

Our journey at Pure Momentum and Athlete University is fundamentally about recognizing that the **sport is the tool, not the destination**. This chapter breaks down our unique operational model and the framework we use to develop the whole child, utilizing their passion—be it soccer, baseball, or any other activity—as the vehicle for success. Our mission is to take children in their formative, sweet-spot ages and provide them with a structured, multifaceted development system that prepares them for life, not just for the next game.

The Foundation: Evolving from a Training Facility to a Licensed Resource Center

The origins of our current model were forged in necessity. When we launched **Pure Momentum LLC** in January 2020, we started as a purely athletic training facility. Our focus was singular: developing athletes. When **COVID-19** hit in March of that year, it triggered a rapid and massive shift. Discretionary income vanished for many families, and the first thing to go was ancillary sports training. To survive and continue serving our community, we accepted an exemption to become an after-school program because we were deemed an **essential service** for working parents.

This pivot wasn't temporary. We took the major step of receiving our certification and paperwork through the **Department of Children and Families (DCF)**, making us a **licensed care provider** through the State of Florida. This transition not only helped us sustain operations but fundamentally changed our mission.

Today, our parent company, Pure Momentum LLC, specializes in development and exposure for student-athletes. **Athlete University** is the physical and philosophical embodiment of that mission. It is our storefront, our operating hub, and also a dual-purpose platform, serving as an online training library for remote or financially constrained athletes. It is a full-time, licensed after-school program, a full summer camp, and a multi-faceted **Student Athlete Resource Center**. We operate under the umbrella of **Pure Momentum Group**, our non-profit arm.

A Day in the Life at Athlete University

We operate as a **licensed care provider**, essentially a specialized daycare for school-age children with an activity- or discipline-based curriculum. It is a place where parents and kids can explore different sports, develop their skill sets, and work on the essential character traits we discussed in previous chapters—like preparation, hard work, and interaction.

The beautiful thing about our approach is that it is not cookie-cutter. Every individual receives what they need based on our varied offerings. Our daily flow is disciplined and efficient:

- **Early Start:** We have an extension program for homeschool kids (often run through programs like Step Up For Students), who come in earlier for socialization and skill-building.
- **After-School Pickup:** Our main after-school program begins with van pickup starting as early as 2:00 PM.
- **Refuel and Focus:** Upon arrival, kids get a healthy snack, and then we immediately tackle **homework**. We allot a specific, controlled amount of time for academics.
- **Controlled Exertion:** The most important part of the afternoon is the **physical activity**. Kids rotate through a discipline activity or athletic training, generally for 45 minutes to an hour. We believe this physical exertion is essential for letting out the aggression and tension built up during the school day.
- **Hard Stop and Responsibility:** At **5:30 PM, it's a hard stop**. Everyone participates in cleanup.

- **Transition:** After cleanup, we transition into parent pickup.

This clean, efficient system becomes second nature for the kids once the standard is set.

Core Elements of Our Framework

Our model is built upon four interconnected and rotating components that work hand-in-hand every day:

1. Development & Skill Acquisition:
- Kids enter at the entry level, trying different activities to identify their interests, temperament, and disposition.
- Once a sport is identified, we focus on **confidence-building** through skill mastery.
- We also incorporate recreational activity (**free play**) where we closely monitor their progress in personal skill development: conflict resolution, teamwork, and social-emotional intelligence.

2. Exposure & Recruitment Services:
- As athletes progress, we provide pathways for **exposure**, which includes showcasing their talents and ultimately navigating the complexities of **college recruitment**.

3. Mentorship & Character Building:

- This is woven into every activity. Our staff guides kids through **conflict resolution** and reinforces positive behavioral standards.

4. Academics & Wellness:
- **Homework** is a non-negotiable first step.
- We provide a **nutritional component**—at least one, often two, healthy snacks—to ensure they have the substance needed for all the activity.

To manage this, we break the kids into groups—"Freshmen," "Sophomores," "Juniors," and "Seniors"—with further sub-groups based on experience. We utilize multiple training zones and stations, creating a constant, efficient rotation so that all children receive their nutritional supplement, complete their homework (if applicable), get their socialization, and understand their duty to clean up, all within the span of three to five days a week.

A Systematic Approach to Building Strong Youth

From a macro perspective, our model is a proven, systematic approach that cities, school districts, and organizations can adopt. We are not creating a new system; we are re-packaging and elevating an existing one.

- **The Regulatory Advantage:** The fact that we are a **DCF-regulated entity is crucial**. We maintain compliance with Level 2 background screenings

for all staff, rigorous log-keeping, incident reports, and healthy practice protocols. This means our model is already a part of the existing governmental structure, making it easily adaptable.
- **Adding Value:** We take that regulated concept and infuse it with immense value by adding a discipline, activity, or passion to the daily routine.
- **The Pivotal Time:** I challenge anyone to find a better use of a child's time between **3:00 PM and 6:00 PM**. This is a pivotal window that is often underutilized.
- **Infrastructure Use:** A core tenet is utilizing resources and facilities that are currently underutilized. Many entities—school boards, cities, counties—already have qualified, able workers (ex-teachers, coaches, counselors) who can staff and manage these programs as standalones or integrated systems.

Our goal is to use the existing infrastructure and systems to revitalize our communities and place our children on an undeniable path to success.

Success Stories: The Proof in the Progress

The true power of this framework is seen in the lives it changes.

- **Jamie:** He was a high-level player with a strong foundation, but he needed our push. He came to us at age 11 or 12 and, just recently at age 17/18, **signed his college scholarship** (or finical agreement, as the system is changing). We helped him across the finish line.

- **Greg:** This younger kid started the year with severe behavioral issues—on an IEP, being violent and aggressive with teachers. I had to step in, go to the school, and help recreate boundaries, teaching him to respond in a way that allows people to hear him. We successfully transitioned him to a different classroom where the "old trauma" was absent. For the last month and a half, he's had **zero incidents**. His whole demeanor and attitude have changed, and he's now able to participate fully.
- **Ed:** He began training with us at 8 years old. Now 18, he has **multiple Division I baseball scholarship offers**. Though he faced political and even racial trials at his school, the framework empowered him to walk through those situations and emerge victorious.
- **Thomas:** A current senior and two-sport star (football and baseball) with scholarship offers from universities like **Tampa, FGCU, Arizona, and Arkansas State**.

The numbers speak for themselves: We currently have over **60 scholarship athletes** across various sports and universities nationwide, and a total of **10 professional athletes** who have come through our system. We are expert navigators of this minefield we call youth development.

The Secret Sauce: Teaching Through Controlled Struggle

If you want to know the secret to the Pure Momentum and Athlete University framework, it is this: We believe in teaching through **controlled struggle**.

We intentionally create carefully curated struggle experiences and scenarios on a daily basis where the kids are sometimes "**behind the eight ball**." We do this to observe and build **resiliency**. Life is about handling challenges, and our program builds:

- The ability to refocus and reset.
- The ability to maintain a positive mindset.
- The ability to talk to yourself with a positive outlook.

By using these experiences to teach them how to struggle, we in turn show these kids how inherently **strong and resilient** they are. This gives them the unshakable confidence of knowing that whatever challenge comes their way, they have a tool for each situation or scenario. We have had tremendous success in equipping them with this **mental and emotional toolkit**.

CHAPTER 6

It's Not a Camp, It's a Sustainable Infrastructure

The biggest mistake people make when evaluating the Pure Momentum Athlete University framework is seeing it as just another after-school camp. It is absolutely **not a camp**. A camp is a temporary event. What we've built is a **sustainable, duplicatable, and systematically governed infrastructure**.

When I talk about infrastructure, I'm referring to a proven model that operates as a **reliable, lasting system**. This system is broken down into distinct, carefully managed components.

The Dual Pillars of Our System

Our program is fundamentally divided into two major operational sides: the **Care Side** and the **Activity Side**. These two sides are interwoven to ensure we provide holistic development.

The Care Side: Nurturing and Compliance

The Care Side focuses on the emotional, physical, and even spiritual maintenance and duty we provide for our participants—our athletes and youth. This aspect is what truly separates us from casual programs.

- **Governing Body:** This side is strictly governed by the **Department of Children and Families (DCF)**, the regulatory body that licenses us as a care provider. We don't try to reinvent the wheel; we rely on DCF to mandate the guidelines, and we build our structure and flexibility around their existing framework. This reliance offers a lot of **stability and credibility** when speaking to city officials, school board members, or parents.
- **Holistic Needs:** We are attentive to all components of a child's well-being, which includes:
  - **Nutrition:** Is the kid eating regularly at home?
  - **Physical and Emotional Health:** Ensuring their physical and emotional needs are met.
  - **Social-Emotional Development:** Teaching them how to interact with counselors, coaches, and peers, and how to deal with issues that arise at home or school.
  - **Transitions:** Addressing issues like transitioning from one activity to the next.
- We also lean heavily on **Step Up For Students**, another governing body that oversees program implementation, especially for initial guidance.

We've found a way to perfectly coincide or fit inside their existing framework.

The Activity Side: Curriculum and Development

This side is where the actual program curriculum lives.

- **Curriculum Focus:** The Activity Side adheres to DCF's intended use for the critical **3:00 to 6:00 PM block**, but we swap out certain traditional elements to fulfill our sports-based mission. We keep the fundamental educational outreach components while layering on a sports and development focus.
- **The Parent Interaction Component:** This is our customer service side, where we engage with parents. We believe in **handling most minor issues in-house**. Parents already have a lot on their plate, so we don't 'dump' every single negative detail on them. If a behavior is a real issue, we bring it to their attention. But things like minor offenses, talking back, or disrespect—which we absolutely do not tolerate—we try to manage in-house, keeping things in proper perspective.

Essential Operational Components

For the entire system to function smoothly as a system, not a camp, we have developed systems that allow us to operate several other crucial facets:

- **Logistics:** This is the operational challenge of moving kids safely—whether it's transporting them from their schools to our facility during the school year or managing field trips and excursions during our summer program.
- **Documentation:** We use systems like **Procare** to track attendance, document arrivals, and keep a daily roll.
- **Compliance:** Ensuring we are in compliance with all rules and regulations set down by our governing bodies, including DCF, the state of Florida, and Step Up For Students.

These systems are why our model is fundamentally a **duplicatable model**. Every community is different, but the core needs of children rarely vary much from city to city or state to state. We can come in, assess the environment, and **tailor our proven system** around that community's needs.

A Duplicatable Model for Maximum Impact

My philosophy is that of an old-school cake maker: I'm a **fundamentalist**. We identify the core ingredients of the after-school model and create a way to duplicate them for continued success.

To make the system duplicatable and sustainable, we follow these steps:

1. **Identify the Target Market:** This is school-age children, typically between 5 and up, with an ideal target of 8 to 12. The need is already apparent because most parents are working during the 3:00 to 6:00 PM window.
2. **Identify and Recruit the Right People:** This is where the real work happens. We need staff with the right **character and moral fiber**. The beauty of our system is that it feeds into an already existing licensing system.
   - We identify existing licensed care providers.
   - We then segment those providers to find individuals with specialized training or a specific discipline we can utilize (like sports coaching).
   - If necessary, we help qualified people start the process of obtaining their licensed care provider credentials, which is a manageable process of continuing education and testing.
3. **Implement Training and Accountability:** We bring in or have the new director job shadow to learn all aspects: parent care, nurturing, activity, logistics, and documentation.
   - We create **templates** for the staff to follow.
   - We institute a daily checklist and a weekly check-in (virtual or in-person) to ensure everyone is aligned.
   - We establish a process of **checks and balances and accountability**.

4. **Continuous Mentorship:** The staff are never more than a phone call away from someone with management experience. **Job shadowing** and ongoing opportunities for staff to run scenarios by experienced mentors—like how to handle a disagreement where one kid pushes another—are essential for continued success. We must give our staff the tools and access to experience so they are equipped to handle any situation.

Going Beyond "Glorified Babysitting"

The greatest misconception that school boards and municipalities have about after-school programs is that they are all just **glorified babysitting**. To be honest, a lot of them are. Many centers lack intrinsic value, discipline, or teaching—they just let kids exist until pickup.

Our Differentiators for Child Success

Our mission is what separates us from the pack. We are not here just to wait on parents. **Everything is a teachable moment**. Our core focus is on raising and nurturing **leadership**.

We instill:

- **Energy, Effort, and Hustle**
- **Passion and Focus**
- **Excitement and Eagerness**
- **Compassion and Empathy**

- **Investment**

We focus on increasing a child's **capacity**, their IQ, and getting them passionate about something. This focus on core individual components puts us in a different stratosphere than traditional centers.

Duplicating the Development

As a former professional athlete and coach, I know that real development is a skillset that must be duplicated. While I may be the driving force or "plug" for coaching, the system doesn't rely solely on me.

- **Identify Specialized Talent:** The challenge is finding people who possess similar real-world, competitive coaching, or playing experience. We must offer **competitive financial compensation** to attract this caliber of leadership—the head coach, the driving force, the engine—someone who never allows their emotions to overpower their intelligence.
- **Trust Your Training:** We create the parameters and allow for flexibility in implementation, but certain core drills and teaching methodologies are staples of the facility. Our motto is, "**Trust your training.**" The kids are expected to trust the training; the coaches are expected to trust the training from their superiors.
- **Strong Leadership, Implementable System:** We provide insight and advice on how to navigate

and select the right personalities, understanding that each environment will take a slightly different skillset.

Funding the Infrastructure: Eliminating Financial Barriers

Any program requires money for facilitation—for staff, supplies, and operations. While the initial funding source is parents paying out-of-pocket, the unique aspect of our licensed model is the ability to tap into already existing societal funding sources.

Tapping into Public Resources

We have the ability to utilize programs like **4C** or **School Readiness** through the Early Learning Coalition. This is a government stipend for after-school care for qualifying families.

- **Addressing the Gap:** A main challenge for many programs is that the kids who need the service most are often the ones whose parents can't afford the cost ($75-$95 a week). Our unique setup allows us to leverage these funds so that **no child is turned away due to financial barriers**. Some parents may pay as little as $5 or $6 a week for access to 12 to 16 hours of quality training—an unbelievable value considering the savings compared to private lessons.

- **Staffing Efficiency:** Our unique model identifies people who have the capacity to serve as both care providers and specialty discipline trainers. This is key to staffing efficiently and maintaining a financial surplus to invest in the program, rather than spending 100 percent of the budget on salaries.
- **Repurposing Assets:** Crucially, for a city or county looking to implement a program like ours, we do not need to ask for new money. **The funds are already existing in the system**. Our request is for already existing resources that are likely underutilized, such as unused school buildings or facilities. We are simply **repurposing the usage of existing assets**.

Building Confidence and Trust

For anyone looking to invest in or implement a program like this, the biggest challenge is overcoming the fear of failure that comes with something seemingly new.

Over-Communicating the Plan

It is essential to understand that you are not starting from scratch; you are leveraging already existing systems like DCF's structure, curriculum, and procedures. This is what you must lean on to guide the process.

It is always better to overcommunicate something simple than to undercommunicate. You must convey the message properly to ensure it is received correctly. This means:

- Go through your plan with a clear business model, addressing all aspects of the system.
- Provide information and tools for external parties (officials, principals, potential partners) to reference the inner workings and to verify that the system works as you claim. You can't simply vouch for yourself; you need **external proof**.

The Foundation of Infrastructure

This is not a camp; it is a continuously operating **infrastructure**. Our planning and activities go beyond the 3:00 to 6:00 PM scope.

- We organize community events like turkey giveaways, backpack drives, and Trunk-or-Treats. The program is built upon this essential **community involvement**.
- Just like a stage performance where the audience sees a polished product but the backstage is a flurry of chaotic activity, the back-end work of logistics, communication, and preparation is the **foundation of our clean, polished product**.

The infrastructure and foundation are key to presenting a sellable and obvious value. At the end of the day, parents must **trust their livelihood or their legacy in your hands**. That is what we are managing, nurturing, and protecting.

CHAPTER 7

The Daily Win: Measuring Short-Term ROI in Youth Development

When we talk about the **Return on Investment (ROI)** for youth development, we must move past abstract concepts and focus on **measurable outcomes**—the tangible proof that our model is working. Part 3 of this book is dedicated to demonstrating that proof through data and observable change. Chapter 7 lays the foundation for this by focusing on the **short-term wins**—the immediate, positive shifts that student-athletes and students experience once they engage with our program's structure.

The very first thing that comes into focus is the daily routine. **Little things equal big things.** To track progress, we first establish a baseline: What is the general tone of the child's morning? Are they prepared? Are they not? We have to take note of these small habits so we can recognize when a shift, adjustment, or transition occurs.

Observing the Initial Shift: Behavior and Attitude

Kids who join our program go through an initial adjustment process. Depending on their personality, this adjustment might manifest as resistance, with them "**beating their chest**," or it might be a quieter, more reclusive period as they try to figure out how to meet our required performance level.

What you start to notice first is a **change in behavior, mood, and attitude**.

- **Interaction:** How do they interact with their immediate circle, like family members? How do they move throughout the day?
- **Conflict Resolution:** How do they deal with conflict or a challenge? Are they sitting in that moment, or are they moving through it? Are they becoming loud and vocal, or quieter and more reclusive?

Our goal is to figure out their baseline attitude and position it to change behavior. This could mean a parent doesn't have to tell them to do the same task as many times.

Another visible change is the natural assumption of a **leadership role**. Because of the interaction and the tempo of our program, many kids begin to take on this role. Initially, that leadership comes from their own activity and preparedness—having good days at school and taking gratification in their accomplishments.

You'll see:

- **Desire for Activity:** They desire more activity and participation with others. They may decide to participate in an extracurricular activity, or they might start drawing more and become less apprehensive about people seeing their work, taking more pride in the things they actually accomplish.
- **A Better Classroom Tone:** From a school or municipal perspective, you'll see immediate wins in the classroom. The overall tone will improve. Kids will clean up after themselves, exhibit more **self-worth and self-value**, and engage in more positive interaction with others, leading to less back-and-forth conflict.
- **Core Values:** They start exhibiting core beliefs and values like saying, "**Yes, sir. No, sir. Please. Thank you.**" These are things we reinforce daily, essentially inputting them into a new internal programming system. As challenges arise, the child now has the ability to see the value and the reason to make a positive decision (Decision A) as opposed to a negative one (Decision B).

The First Measurable Change: Self-Awareness to Accountability

If we are being completely transparent, the first measurable change that stands out is **self-awareness**.

The student finally becomes aware of their actions and realizes that their environment is often shared with others from different households, cultures, and backgrounds. The key question we get them to internalize is: **Am I having a positive or negative impact on my environment?** Are my actions allowing others to be healthy, happy, and well-adjusted, or am I preventing someone from getting what they need to be successful? This **awareness** of how their actions affect others is the crucial first step.

The way that self-awareness translates to the individual is **accountability**. For many of these kids, this is their introduction to the concept.

It's vital to make a point of emphasis here: **Do not confuse responsibility with accountability**.

- **Responsibility** comprises the things that other people can identify as being yours—tasks you are responsible for achieving.
- **Accountability** is the awareness that these things are yours and that you are actively holding yourself accountable for accomplishing them.

We focus on accountability because many people are responsible for tasks but lack the internal drive to hold themselves accountable, so those things simply don't get done. Accountability is the foundation of awareness that allows us to move throughout our day, stay task-oriented, and interact with others in a polite, helpful manner where we are an asset, not a liability.

The power of this awareness is the ability to **step outside of oneself** in the moment and take an account of whether their current actions are serving a positive mindset or something negative. For a kid between the ages of 8 and 12, that alone is profound as a building block for their life journey.

Bridging the Gap: From Awareness to Production

So, how do we bridge the gap from awareness to actual production? We see this self-awareness in how they interact with others daily—how they greet their family, or how they deal with conflict. **Struggle and stress teach us and show us our character.**

Self-awareness quickly lends itself to a **higher moral standard or high character.** Things that would have been major hurdles before are now moved through quickly. They take more accountability and responsibility in their schoolwork, their appearance, and in ensuring they are prepared for the next day by using tools like writing in a planner. These activities further the awareness of, "**Am I meeting the day, or is the day meeting me?**"

This transition leads directly to **better focus** and ultimately, **higher, better performing grades**. Teachers and counselors will notice this fundamental shift in awareness and take note of it. The student will receive positive notes, affirmations, and lots of gratification because they are now exhibiting this self-aware, high-character behavior. This effect continues to trickle down into all other aspects of their life.

Defining Increased Engagement

When measuring ROI, one of the key data points is **increased engagement**. From our perspective, engagement is defined as **initiating positive contact and providing positive feedback**.

The core of positive engagement is seen in the following:

- **Self-Initiation:** Are they waking themselves up? Are they aware of the set of tasks they need to accomplish to get from point A to point B?
- **Positive Communication:** Are they initiating positive things with people? Saying, "Good morning," or "How was your day?" Are they asking, "Is there anything I could do for you?"
- **The Give and Receive:** We require our kids to do something nice for someone and to ask if someone did something nice for them. This makes them aware of the concept of the give and the reciprocating receive. It says, "**I am a person who will engage in a positive manner, and I expect people to engage me in a positive manner.**"

Engagement is simply how we are meeting our environment. Are we initiating positive experiences with our homework, extracurricular activities, or even with complying with our parents' wishes? We want them to initiate positive contact with their environment and to expect to receive positive engagement in return.

Strategies for Activating the Inactive Child

To get an inactive kid active again, our go-to strategy is to give them **more responsibility**.

A quick story: We had a kid, **Henry**, who lacked passion, energy, and excitement for anything other than watching a tablet. We started by giving him responsibilities that empowered him and gave him confidence:

- "Henry, check the book bags and let me know how many aren't on hooks."
- "Henry, check the trash cans and let me know when they're overfilled."
- "Henry, make sure all the balls are picked up at the end of the day."

This responsibility gave him a place and a role, and he started to look forward to it. Once this was established, we started the slow concept of **stacking**. We would say, "Hey Henry, go check the trash cans, and then I want you to run three laps because I want to work on your speed."

We want them to be passionate first about **leadership**, which we define as being a **great follower first**.

1. **Be a Great Follower:** Once you are a great follower, whoever is the leader will allow you to lead a subset group because you are a great example.

2. **Be a Great Listener:** From being a great follower, you become a great listener.
3. **Be a Great Example:** Now, the leader can refer other people to you to watch your actions.

We then take that foundation and start to identify **confidence** before transitioning that confidence into **discipline**.

The Power of Acknowledged Progression

We are not just talking about abstract measurables. The proof is in the progression:

Student Example	Starting Point	Measurable Short-Term Win	Progression/Result
Charles	Not playing any extracurricular activity.	**Increased Activity & Drive**	In less than a year, he went from non-participation to playing basketball at our facility, then requesting to play in city leagues, and is now pursuing competitive AAU basketball.

Student Example	Starting Point	Measurable Short-Term Win	Progression/Result
Sarah	Not an athlete.	**Tangible Performance Improvement**	Played baseball, transitioned to softball, and her mom reported her batting average increased by 150 points in one season. She made the All-Star team and now wants to play basketball.
Jaylen	High-performing player on JV team (9th grade).	**Leadership & Elevated Performance**	Became the star shortstop and captain of the Varsity team (AA high school) as a sophomore.
Kiera	Good kid, stayed in her lane, low social impact.	**External Acknowledgment & Self-Worth**	Received the **"Warrior of the Month"** award at school for exemplifying positive characteristics.

Student Example	Starting Point	Measurable Short-Term Win	Progression/ Result
Grayson	Super shy, refused to engage with people.	**Increased Confidence & Communication**	Through daily required interaction, he went from not talking to working in groups, and recently gave an unprompted speech in class about his weekend vacation.

We find that **85 to 90 percent** of our kids transition into some kind of disciplined extracurricular or sport activity. It's just what we do. While we are fundamentally and core-principle based, when all these things align—the energy, effort, attitude, hustle, and passion—the numbers will reflect it.

Another crucial short-term win is **acknowledgement from adults outside of the immediate family circle**. We have had kids receive "Good Samaritan" or "Best Helper" awards. When this gratification and acknowledgement comes from outside the circle, it reaffirms and co-signs the fact that, "**Hey, I'm moving on the right track.**" This gives the youth a tremendous boost of confidence because they know the personal development journey is paying off.

We always teach them: **Accountability is it**. No matter what happened, whether it was good, bad, or indifferent, you have to take responsibility for the things that are happening in your life. From taking that responsibility and being accountable, we can now be **intentional**, and that is the overall goal. The short-term wins are the steps that build the path toward that intentional life.

CHAPTER 8

The Midterm Proof of Academic Improvement

Chapter 8 focuses on the midterm return on investment that comes in the form of **academic improvement**. When we look for this midterm success, we're asking: Is our structured approach translating into real, tangible results in the classroom? The answer is a resounding yes, and I want to paint a picture of why.

Imagine a single mom of two. She's working double shifts, a superhero in her own right, but like all of us, her time is limited. Providing for her family must take precedence over standing in in some other important areas. Then, she gets the call: a parent-teacher conference. Her kids aren't performing well; they aren't spending enough time on concepts. This isn't due to a lack of desire—it's just kids being kids, and the necessary time and guidance aren't happening.

Now, this mom can't afford tutoring in all these different subjects. She's truly between a rock and a hard place. A friend refers her to Athlete University. She brings her kids in, she tours the facility, meets the director and the staff, and sees how they engage. Crucially, she observes our **homework help session**, where two or three staff members are actively walking through the space, helping kids with homework at specific times.

Systematizing Accountability and Discipline

We sat down with this mom and explained that the biggest thing we have to do is identify where the weaknesses are. This is where we implement a crucial system of **accountability and discipline**.

The system is simple, but powerful:

- As soon as the children arrive, they must pull out their planners and any graded work that was returned.
- All graded work must be handed over.

Initially, accountability isn't an internal, self-motivated thing for every child, especially when they're dealing with emotions of inferiority, lack, or uncertainty. Sometimes, that accountability has to be put in place—it has to be in the form of an **accountability partner**. In this scenario, our facility, Athlete University, steps in to become that mentor, tutor, and second guardian. We ensure the kids are doing what they're supposed to do on a daily basis.

Through this persistent, systematic approach—by being upfront, accountable, and intentional—we've seen a number of our kids go from not performing well to **performing at a high level** just by the structure we provide during that critical **3:00 to 6:00 PM** time frame.

Simulating Success Through Micro-Doses of School

Our core goal during that after-school time is to **simulate school in micro-doses**. We aim to galvanize and intensify the specific skill sets needed to be successful in life.

For example, we transition from physical activity — which is good for dumping that excess pent-up energy accumulated from being in class — to our tutoring/homework session.

The Homework and Struggle Dynamic

We establish a baseline for new kids to understand their school's specific workload, since every school and teacher is different. Once that is understood, every kid is expected to present their homework.

We run this session in a group-style format, with staff members helping as issues arise. Here's a core tenant of our philosophy: we instruct all of our staff to **allow the children to sit in that struggle for a while**. We don't want them to be saved the moment they encounter trouble. We want them to build up a tolerance and a natural defense for struggle. We want them to embrace the challenge and understand, "Hey, this is something you are capable of doing."

This is also where **follow-through and respect** come into play. We had one of our younger kids lie about having homework. When the truth came out, they had to "**pay the piper**" — the head coach, the general, steps in and implements discipline in a way that allows everyone to know why the child is being disciplined. If there's no follow-through, there will be no respect.

Leveraging Time Constraints and Control

Crucially, we do not give **unlimited time** for homework. Everything has a time frame (typically 30–45 minutes). Why? Because we believe that physical interaction is just as important as doing the homework at that moment.

By giving them those **time constraints** and ensuring they understand that everything has a time and place, we've found that they work more diligently. They stop taking the victim approach or victim role and become motivated and challenged to do the work.

The fact that we operate this school-like format in a setting that is **not handicapped by legislation and doctrine** gives us the advantage and the leverage. We have things the kids want that we can withhold — snack, playtime, pizza on Fridays. If a kid refuses to do their math homework in our environment, they might have to go out and run until they decide they're ready. This micro-school concept gives them extra practice on how to move through different situations and allows them to be managed by professionals who understand how to move a kid from one moment to the next.

The Pattern of Structure and Focus

We are all creatures of habit, and kids even more so. The continuous **structure and daily routine** we provide doesn't leave much room for deviation. We attempt to control their activity through a focused, guided, structured curriculum. Every moment of the day is supposed to be doing something.

Even in leisure activities, we are always making **focus** a focal point.

For instance, we did a team-building exercise where we put kids in pairs: one partner was blindfolded but could hear, and the other could see and talk. We threw tennis balls around (a "minefield"), and the seeing partner had to navigate the blindfolded partner through it. This activity breaks the norm, but it also forces them to realize:

- How to **communicate and receive messages**.
- How two people can see the same thing but say it differently.

In this activity, we were actively **increasing their focus**. Our belief is that everyone has an attention span, and our goal is to increase that attention span slowly over time through guided activity. We know that attention span is often determined by the child's level of excitement in that discipline. Knowing this, we can begin the process of expanding their attention span slowly.

From IEP to Independence: The Story of Chance

I can absolutely tell you about a student we'll call **Chance**. Chance came to us on an **IEP (Individualized Education Program)**. His issue was more physical, but the physical outbursts led to a perceived issue that was mental—something out of his control.

I had never sat in on an IEP meeting before, but I was allowed to attend one with the parent. The tone of the meeting, in my opinion, wasn't the best—the parent felt responsible and judged, and the child, though not addressed directly, was still in the room listening. I laid the groundwork: I explained my role and what I saw in Chance in a different environment where he was exhibiting success. My goal was simple: How do we create an environment where we can have some expected consistency from the child's productivity?

I suggested switching the child's primary teacher, thinking that perhaps there was so much trauma there that neither side could let go. Sometimes, certain environments—oil and water—just don't mix, and it's our job to rectify that. The initial move was denied, as IEPs have a paper trail and channels they must follow. Progressively, things got worse. By March, the mom was afraid they would ask him to repeat the grade because he was missing so much class time.

Finally, in the middle of March, they moved the kid to a new teacher. The change wasn't 180 degrees overnight, but the new teacher didn't have a stored-up negative mindset about the kid. When he did mess up, it wasn't anticipated, and it wasn't met with an energy that would antagonize or exacerbate the situation.

Because of this shift, **Chance's IEP was removed**, and he was allowed to move on to the next grade without summer school. Considering that Chance had gone through the trauma of losing a parent who was murdered, we consider this a **tremendous win**.

Our goal is not to judge; our goal is to get **results**. A big part of what we do is **protecting the teachers by providing them with a resource**. We're not just saying the teacher is the problem, but we are acknowledging that sometimes a simple change of environment is what's best for that child. Our unbiased, day-to-day work allows us to bring a fresh, respected perspective to the situation.

Misconceptions and Mindset of the Student-Athlete

There are some common misconceptions about connecting athletics and academics that we work hard to debunk.

Debunking Common Misconceptions

Misconception	Our Reality
"Great athlete = Great student"	Neither this nor its opposite are inherently true. Success is individual-based.
"Sports and academics don't feed each other."	We draw direct correlations: the preparation and preparedness habits used for athletic success must be **emulated and mimicked in the classroom**.
"All athletes are jocks who get passed along."	A large majority of athletes are actually held to a **higher standard**, sometimes unfairly. Some people dislike the access and notoriety they're given.
"It's easy being a student-athlete."	It's one of the most difficult things I ever did. You're working a job without getting paid. The time commitment is immense and builds character.

Overcoming Misconceptions: Mindset and System

We prepare the athlete to overcome these challenges through two primary areas: **mindset and systematic infrastructure**.

1. Mindset: Preparedness Meets Opportunity

We tell our kids, "It's better to be lucky than be good." But we immediately follow that with the old adage: Luck is when preparedness meets opportunity.

Our mindset is: **It's me against the world**. Just because you choose to be a student-athlete doesn't mean anyone else is going to give you any credit. You are simply choosing to do more. This is where **awareness and accountability** return to the forefront.

- No one owes you the benefit of the doubt.
- You owe yourself the opportunity to put your best foot forward.

When you put **preparation, energy, effort, attitude, hustle, and passion** on the forefront, there is no room for the acknowledgment of someone not liking who you choose to be. We coach them through realizing that they have the power to **not let someone else define their self-esteem**.

2. Infrastructure: Scheduled Accountability

The infrastructure we provide is all about scheduling. Especially for a student-athlete whose time is very short, we schedule every moment of the day.

- **Personal Development Time:** We do an exercise where we look at the 24 hours in a day to identify where their time to separate themselves from their peers will come from. For most kids, this is the **3:00 to 6:00 PM** time frame. If you're a high school student-athlete, this time is often dedicated to team practice. This is why we have to be rigorous.

My personal mandate to my own daughter is: **Before you do anything that's not going to add to who you are to become as a person, you must do something that is going to build a skill set.** If not, the child will always lend themselves to comfortability. **Growth only happens through uncomfortability.**

Our systematic approach is built on:

- **Planner Use:** We get them a planner and have them document all homework, school obligations, practice time, and even downtime (like a birthday party). Their planner acts as their calendar.
- **Intolerance for Inactivity:** We do not accept "I don't know" as an acceptable answer.
- **Tears Are Not Currency:** We do not accept crying as currency for getting out of a consequence. We coach them to have a safe outlet but to not sit in despair, sulking in pity.

This structure creates **expectations in themselves**. Without structured discipline and preparedness, there can be no expectation.

The Recipe for Replicating Our System

For any entity—a school, city, or organization—interested in modeling our system, the most important concept is **leadership**. Attitude will always reflect leadership.

1. Identify Discipline-Focused Leadership

The Director of the program and the Head Coach (which I suggest should be two different people) must be:

- **Discipline-focused, driven, and goal-oriented.**
- People of a certain station, meaning they've led, run a business, managed others, or been an athlete.
- **Not focused on being liked.** Their purpose is to convey the truth in a way that everyone is aware of what's expected.

If you've never been responsible or held accountable for someone else's actions, you don't truly understand what **fairness** means. Fairness is not about everyone receiving equal treatment; it means everyone is fully aware of the standard and has someone who takes responsibility for making sure everyone follows the guidelines. **Fairness is enacted when everyone is held to the same standard**.

2. Implement a Structured, Trigger-Aware Curriculum

The bulk of the system is a scheduled curriculum. The day is broken down into three main segments:

- **Preparation (1.5 hours prior):** Van logging, administrative tasks, cleaning, systems.
- **Logistics and Transition:** Getting the kids, logging them in, putting up book bags.
- **The Curriculum:** Homework session, transition to activities.

We also have to identify personalities that don't go well together ("oil and vinegar") and avoid activities that might bait them into negative behavior. We must know each kid's **triggers**. When the energy shifts or the kids lose focus, our tool is to immediately transition into another activity, offering a new challenge and recalibrating their attention.

Conclusion: The Transformative Investment

The reality is, much of the skill building and character development that is not done at home—because parents are exhausted or obligated—is being taught in our system. The lessons that life teaches that you don't learn in school are now being provided through high-level training and development.

This is a **controlled narrative** we act out each day, where we know how our program responds to their actions—the curriculum is the standard. An investment in this model means a school or city is bringing in a partner that specializes in the development of young people.

The children who participate are going back into school with:

- More real-life, life application training.
- The ability to handle scenarios in a positive manner.

They've been allowed to fail and learn in a structured, controlled environment, just as Michael Jordan became the best not because he never failed, but because he failed more than everyone else, unseen. It's truly transformative.

To receive a return on investment (ROI), you must be willing to invest or trust and then invest. We all want to know what the return will be, but I leave you with this question: **What are you willing to invest to receive the return on the investment?** It's not just money or time; sometimes, it requires parents to sit down and receive information on how to better the situation. We are all a part of this process.

CHAPTER 9

The Immeasurable Return: Cultivating Options, Not Just Athletes

When we talk about the long-term results of our framework—Pillar 3 of our model—we are focused squarely on the measurable **return on investment (ROI)** in terms of long-term success. But the true ROI isn't a single, static number; it's a **compounding effect** that opens up a world of **choices** for our young people.

I want you to hold a picture in your mind: that 18-year-old kid. He's the product of a single-parent home. He's about to make his way into the world, but the difference this time is that he has been nurtured through a system specifically designed to get him to this point. There's no "feel-sorry for him." It's not a sad story. It's not the what could have been or the what if. Everything is ahead of him, and he's looking forward to the challenge.

The Power of Choice

Consider a quick story. Let's call him **Brett**. Brett was 13, a product of a single-parent home. He was talented, but unguided. He found the program, and he was nurtured, inspired, reprimanded, disciplined, loved, challenged, and supported. 5 years later, he's finishing his senior year. He calls me up and says, "Hey UNC, I got this scholarship offer (financial agreement) to the University of Tampa. They want me to come play baseball there."

At this moment, the narrative switches from, "What are you going to do?" to **"What do you want to do?"**

I think that's where the emphasis of this chapter lies: **Options**. The primary goal of the program is to give all of our students and athletes options. So many times, children don't have options. They feel boxed in, "I have to do this because it's the only thing I can do," or, "I need to go get a job." Now, they can actually continue their growth and continue to grow in different ways, whether it be in college, secondary education, or athletics. This gives them more life experiences. Empowering student-athletes with the **option of choice** is the ultimate win.

Impact Beyond the Numbers

When I look back and realize we've helped support over **60 athletes get college scholarships**, the first word that comes to mind is **impact**. Measurable, meaningful impact.

That number represents over 60 sentient beings out there in the world with a belief, who have been empowered and nurtured. They've been raised on a similar cocktail; they are part of a new family structure. It's crazy to think, but many of them don't even know each other exist, yet they are all part of the same fabric.

The number 60 is not the end goal, but it is a data point that tells us we are fulfilling the mission. Our aim was not to become large company. It was always about impact. That number means we are on the right path and the right track. It's a great feeling to step back and realize that so many kids have been positively impacted, and that every year, we continue to have kids going off to college. This is **true, unquantifiable impact**, and no one can take that away from us.

Defining Life Success Outside the Box

We are preparing young people not just for athletic success, but for **life success**. The reality is that success isn't linear. What's success to you doesn't necessarily equate to success for me, and vice versa. It's an ever-changing, ever-evolving concept, much like how they say, "Beauty is in the eye of the beholder."

Most kids need help along the way. Even kids from two-parent homes often have something missing—that firm, consistent voice that will always be true to them.

Here is a real example of life success outside of sports:

Case Study: Thomas, the 3 Hole Hitter

Thomas was a tremendous student-athlete and a phenomenal baseball player. He could flat-out hit. But his structure wasn't traditional, and he lacked early guidance.

After high school, he didn't go the traditional route. He didn't go to college. He bounced around, working as a local DJ, selling solar, and now he's working in finance.

I recently reached out to him about renting our facility for an event, knowing he was still in the party scene. He connected me with his contacts, and we are now working through a contract for a series of events.

Thomas is not playing baseball; he didn't go to college, but the kid is **successful**.

I had a conversation with Thomas recently where he was apprehensive about starting a new job—uncharted territory. I told him, "Man, listen, remember this: **You are a three hole hitter, bro.**"

In baseball, batting 3rd in the line up means everyone knows you are capable and everyone is expecting you to make an adjustment.

"You've always made the adjustment," I told him. "**Even though you're behind the eight ball, you've always been able to figure out a way to get it done.** Don't worry about what you don't know. Just show up and compete, because that's the true essence of who you are."

It was a deeply meaningful conversation that had absolutely nothing to do with sports and everything to do with his **ability to adjust, adapt, and compete in life.**

The Vehicle, Not the Journey: Building Identity

Our foundational philosophy is: **Sports is the vehicle, not the journey.**

We are using sports as a tool to create the student's **future avatar**. It's all about where we want to be and who we have to become to carry the success we desire.

An affirmation I use, which is good for anyone, is: **"What do I need to understand to create the future that I desire?"**

To achieve something, you must possess a certain knowledge base, skillset, and IQ level in that discipline. Through our day-to-day life and experiences in the program, we are creating capacity and equipping them with the skills necessary to adjust to life's challenges.

We infuse a specific, non-negotiable mindset:

- **Accountability**
- **Positivity**
- **Capability**
- **Adaptability**
- **Toughness**

We teach them that **"The best ability is availability."** We aim to be the most dependable piece of the puzzle.

When people can depend on you, you have leverage, and you can monetize that skillset. This lends itself to preparation, being present, being adaptable, and being a great teammate in any setting—sports, the classroom, or the workplace.

The kids who go through our program are **battle-tested**. Keeping with the theme of 3:00 PM to 6:00 PM being the battlefield, we challenge these kids daily. We are intentionally making them struggle and work through processes so that their:

- **Problem-solving**
- **Conflict resolution**
- **Focus**
- **Critical thinking**

...are all on par, ready for the next level and phase of life. The reality is, **we learn and grow through struggle**.

The Ever-Evolving ROI

The goal of any program is to have meaningful impact and help mold polished, well-rounded members of society. We want them to be assets and to be impactful. We have a proven track record of producing products that are valuable assets and leaders.

They are leaders not in the sense of telling people what to do, but in being an **example** of what to do on a day-to-day basis. They understand and accept expectations, they are accountable to the work, and they prepare for the job. When they fall short, they don't make excuses; they take responsibility and accountability for their actions.

Here are some of the tools we use to drive this long-term success:

- **Formal Preparation:** We run **college tours** and provide robust **SAT/ACT prep**. We don't just "run them out there"; we prepare them so they understand the context of what they are about to face.
- **Real-World Application:** We have them participate in **community service**. They understand terms like outreach, social service, and investment because they live them.
- **The Business of Me Personal Development Course:** This is an eight-week online offering for middle and high school students. We bring in different speakers each week to discuss:
  - Hygiene and Etiquette
  - Conflict Resolution
  - Social Media and Investment
- **Athletes Guiding Athletes (AGAs):** This program puts our scholarship athletes in a **mentoring role** via virtual platforms, where they can interact with and mentor our younger athletes. They are raised in a culture of helping.

The ROI is difficult to quantify because it's ever-evolving and ever-changing. The kids who get scholarships will go on to do great things, save lives, and impact others. They will, themselves, help people get scholarships because that's the culture they were raised in. The effect is being **compounded daily** by their growth and maturity.

To the patron who is looking to quantify this ROI: understand that you are the initial piece of it. The return on investment has a large part to do with the patron's **initial willingness to invest** and their mindset in going into that investment. You have to be willing to invest to receive a return. We provide the mechanism for an immense, unquantifiable, and ever-growing yield.

CHAPTER 10

Funding the Mission: Tapping into Existing Family Resources

As we embark on Part 4, "**The Institutional Playbook: The Macro Solution**," my goal is to provide a clear path for decision-makers—from parents to school administrators—on how to practically adopt this system. This chapter focuses specifically on "**Funding the Mission: Tapping into Existing Family Resources**" because, ultimately, a lack of funding should never be the excuse that stops a child from reaching their potential.

When we talk about how this program gets paid for, the reality is there are a multitude of ways that it gets funded, and we are structured to tap into all of them. Our philosophy is to exist in an area where there are **no excuses**. We identify the need, and then we position ourselves with the paperwork, certifications, and licensing to find a funding source for those who are motivated and interested.

Leveraging Income-Based Subsidies: The 4C Model

One of the primary ways this program is funded is through parents' out-of-pocket costs, as it is, at its core, a childcare and development service. However, a significant portion of families qualify for **existing income-based resources** that can cover the expense.

A prime example is the **School Readiness program**. This initiative, often overseen by the Early Learning Coalition (ELC), focuses on getting children a healthy start through programs like Head Start and Kindergarten. In Florida, they offer a specific program called **4C (Child Care)**, which is an income-based subsidy available nationwide under similar names and structures.

Here's how we utilize this existing infrastructure:

- **The Qualification:** The program uses a **sliding scale** based on a family's income. Parents must meet a set of criteria, such as having a job (filing a 1099 or a W2) or being a student.
- **Our Certification:** What makes our program unique and differentiates us is that we are a **licensed care provider through DCF** (Department of Children and Families) or the equivalent state agency. This means we are in line, based on our certifications, to receive this **government stipend**.
- **The Process:** The parent applies directly to the ELC/4C. Once qualified, they receive a stipend that can be directed to any qualified center they

choose—including ours. The funds are then used to manage the actual care and development of the child.

This mechanism is a game-changer for many families, especially those in inner-city communities, whose discretionary income wouldn't normally allow for these types of auxiliary developmental programs. It offers **tremendous value** because the child is not only being cared for during crucial after-school hours but is also being stimulated and developed in different athletic and academic disciplines. Where other after-school programs or daycares exist, we use these funds to actively train and teach discipline and structure.

We proactively help parents navigate this process by hosting **informationals** where we'll get a group together, bring laptops, and walk them through the 4C application process.

Additional Funding Avenues for Families

Beyond 4C, there are several other programs and strategic approaches we leverage to ensure funding isn't a blocker:

- **Step Up for Students:** In Florida, this is a private school scholarship fund that allows parents who opt for homeschooling or private school to receive aid. This is another certification we maintain, which aids parents who may not have the

discretionary income but have access to these resources.
- **Dual Compliance (Non-profit/For-profit):** Our program operates with a **dual compliance model**—as a non-profit and as a for-profit entity. This positions us to receive:
  - Grants for betterment, education, tutoring, wellness, technology, and art. We are constantly applying for these.
  - Donations from foundations that align with our mission.
- **Health and Wellness Resources:** We are currently exploring opportunities through programs like **Medicare**, where resources can be afforded to children based on health and wellness for healthy living and education through exercise and Telehealth.

Addressing the Biggest Funding Barrier: The Budget

When looking at the funding challenges faced by families and schools, it always comes down to **budgetary allocation**—dollars and cents.

The biggest barrier for parents is **discretionary income**. We all have unlimited needs and wants but limited resources. Parents allocate funds on a need-by-need basis: household expenses, rent, food, clothing, and transportation. Developmental and extracurricular activities, while vital, don't take precedence over food, water, clothing, or shelter. These activities are usually associated with that flexible, discretionary income, and they are often the first things that get pushed to the back burner.

What we urge parents and community leaders to realize is that this program is an **investment in the community, in the child, and in your legacy**. These are the future teachers, leaders, and doctors.

From a school district's perspective, the barrier is the same: how do we find the resources to invest in something that doesn't strictly qualify as a need but directly correlates to a student's success and the ability to become a well-rounded individual?

The fix we implemented, which solidifies the mission and justifies the request, is placing our program in the **3 p.m. to 6 p.m. window**. This time frame inherently justifies the allocation of funds because it fills a void where parents need coverage and guidance for their children. It turns a "want" (developmental training) into a justifiable **necessity** (after-school childcare and supervision).

Navigating the "Gray Area" of Income and Qualification

One of the toughest financial situations is the two-parent household where both parents work and bills are paid, but they make too much money to qualify for programs like 4C, yet have zero discretionary income left over. They are constantly struggling financially, sitting in a funding **"gray area."**

For these families, the solution starts with **communication and creativity**.

The Communication Barrier
Money conversations are sensitive. The biggest issue we face is a **lack of open dialogue** because parents often don't want to share all of their financial details. This is especially true in minority communities (Black, Hispanic, Asian, Latino) where there is a tendency to keep finances private. We must foster an open environment to find a viable solution.

Creative Funding Solutions
- **Strategic Qualification:** Just because a family assumes they won't qualify for a governmental program doesn't mean they won't. Some options allow for one parent to be designated as the primary guardian for the paperwork, which can bring the household income down a notch for the purposes of that specific program. These government program qualifications are separate from IRS filings.
- **External Sponsorships:** We always have grant money available, and we actively take donations and sponsors. Parents can also be encouraged to find their own sponsors—a local business, a foundation, or other entities—that would offset the cost. Since we are a non-profit, we are in line to accept donations for scholarships for disadvantaged kids.

- **Referral Programs:** Depending on the situation, we may defer certain costs in exchange for the parent helping us market and advertise, getting the word out, or leveraging their network for resources that benefit the program.

Institutional Investment and Partnership with Schools

Schools are a critical part of the macro solution. There is absolutely an opportunity for schools to invest in their students through this model; the cost does not have to be entirely deferred to the parents.

The most effective approach is a **strategic partnership**:

- **Satellite Site Operation:** We can come in and run a **satellite site** directly from the school's facility. We utilize their classrooms, gym, and playground spaces for the educational curriculum and program activities.
- **Logistical Support:** We handle the logistics, such as transporting kids for parents who need it.
- **District-Level Scholarship:** The school district can choose to cover some costs for students who qualify, or simply grant the program access to students who would benefit.
- **Giveback Model:** We can create a formal partnership with a giveback component, often in the form of increasing the number of registrations or

scholarships granted to students who could not qualify or whose parents could not afford the program.

There is tremendous flexibility in this model, allowing us to sit down with the school or district and work out the details that align with their specific budgetary and student needs.

Common Mistakes Administrators Make

The key to successful implementation and funding lies in strategic partnership and narrative.

- **Mistake 1: Poor Personnel and Partnership Selection.** Administrators often fail to identify the right type of individual or organization to implement the program. This isn't a short lever; it's a long-term play. The partner must be a big-picture, detail-oriented person with structure and organization. More importantly, administrators are bound by various restraints and restrictions, so they must partner with entities that have the correct **certification, paperwork, and licensing** to support the work. We are already a licensed partner with multiple County School Boards, which provides an instant credibility for our track record and compliance.
- **Mistake 2: Lacking a Compelling Narrative for Funding.** Seeking funding is about networking

and creating the proper platform and narrative. Administrators must clearly articulate why they need the funds and what they will do with them, which requires a certain amount of transparency. The mistake is often that they are too close to the project, creating a perception of conflict of interest. The solution is finding the right organization—one with a deep community presence—to convey the message. The perception must be that a resource is coming in to offer resources, not that a business is coming in simply to make money. Our existing community outreach efforts (like teach-in days, tech days, and community events) already provide the necessary trust and track record.

Conclusion: The Responsibility of Action

To whom much is given, much is expected. Parents, city officials, administrators, and teachers all have a tremendous responsibility, and sometimes the sheer weight of that responsibility prevents action.

The biggest step is to simply go and look at people who are actively running these programs to understand the real need on the ground. At the end of the day, **togetherness is what creates opportunity**. This entire system is about the kids—it's about instilling a sense of passion, pride, integrity, and confidence in them so they can become well-rounded, productive members of society.

This resource is not just our tool; it's the world's resource. I urge all stakeholders—parents, administrators, and city officials—to read the book, ask the hard questions, and come out for site visits so we can begin implementing these programs right away.

CHAPTER 11

Institutional Partnerships: Aligning with Schools and Districts

When offering any kind of insight or perspective to career educators and institutional leaders, the first thing that must be addressed is the magnitude of their responsibility. This commitment should not be taken lightly. We must step back and give proper, just due—or give flowers—to those people who have made a **lifelong commitment to the youth**. Decisions made at the institutional level carry tremendous weight, and I want to start by acknowledging and saying, "**Thanks for the commitment, the service, and the way you selflessly commit your talents and efforts to young people.**"

Now, moving forward, it's important to understand the fundamental skills that place institutional leaders where they are: they can **organize, delegate, and compartmentalize**. My goal in this chapter is to show how **partnering** with outside entities—individuals and organizations that may not be on the institutional side—can be a key component in driving continued success and achieving the measurable goals for each district or institution.

Building Trust and Transparency

We spoke earlier about the importance of getting the right people in the room. This initial meeting, where every decision-maker is present, is vital. You don't want anyone to have any momentum over anybody else. It is a given that our group will be coming in with a certain amount of energy and passion—a certain amount of wind behind our sales.

Therefore, the biggest objective in this first interaction is to create a level of **transparency, trust, and commonality**. At the end of the day, we are all leaders of young people, and the goal is figuring out how we can use each other's talents and resources to create more opportunities for these children, whether they are student-athletes or simply students.

To create that bond and structure, we initiate a process that includes:

- A **walk-through or tour** of the facility, allowing leaders to see the operational environment.
- An initial meeting where we thoroughly discuss our **pitch deck**. We have a presentation specifically geared toward municipalities, cities, and institutions.

- Ensuring every potential decision-maker is in the room so that everyone gets a feel for each other's personality, tone, and motives. This allows everyone to feel good about moving forward together.

Leveraging National Programs: The 21st Century Model

It is crucial for districts and our program to understand how we can align with existing resource structures, such as **21st Century Community Learning Centers**.

The 21st Century organization offers after-school program resources to qualifying children in specific areas, often mirroring empowerment zones or Title I zones. They fund and operate these programs, hiring vendors and staff for both educational and recreational activities.

How We Integrate with 21st Century Programs

The biggest initial advantage we offer is our **compliance status**. Since we are **DCF regulated and DCF licensed** (Department of Children and Families), our model is qualified to go into any 21st Century after-school program or one that is funded through it.

Because we are licensed and certified, our staff can walk right in and **work in unison**. We have the same background screening requirements, the same level of tools, and an identical structure and compliance standard to what the institution already maintains. This immediate qualification removes a **significant barrier to partnership**.

The Superintendent's Launch Playbook

If a superintendent wants to launch a program similar to ours, my advice involves a structured, multi-step process focused on intentional selection, clear vision, and community integration.

Seven Steps to Launch

1. **In-Person Walk-Through and Key Meeting:** First, I would request an in-person meeting and walk-through. This should include all personnel integral to the endeavor, such as the secretary, the person with an athletic background, the childcare expert, or the accountant. We need everyone who will be involved in the execution.
2. **Identify the Cornerstones:** Select and inform the two core cornerstones: the **Director and the Head Coach** (or the "general," if you will). These individuals will be central to everything you build.
3. **Strategic Staff Recruiting:** Use existing institutional and school system resources to identify and recruit staff who possess the perfect balance of essential character traits: organizational structure, assertiveness, positivity, and being a disciplinarian. These traits must permeate the entire staff.

4. **Define the Center's Vision (Curating Experience):** Determine the specific vision for this unique center. Every location has the ability to be unique. We can curate different experiences and opportunities. What are the core programs you want to offer? Do you want this center to focus on coding and tennis? Golf and baseball? Basketball and football? Defining the core programming allows us to select staff and resources accordingly.
5. **Location, Location, Location:** Decide on the physical space. Are you sharing existing school space during off-hours, or is there an unused building or resource that can be **repurposed**? We always want to be good stewards of land and resources already allocated but not currently utilized.
6. **Introducing the Concept:** Introduce the new concept to the populace—the parents and kids. This can be done via a **block party or an informational meeting** where we offer resources and assess the makeup of the group.
7. **Dress Rehearsals:** Conduct a few **dress rehearsals**. Invite parents and kids to go through a "dress rehearsal after-school program day." This gives them a chance to see what it would be like while also providing insight into the procedures and structures we put in place to ensure long-term success.

Empowering Institutional Power Sharers

The youth of today are not the kids of old; they are not us, or previous generations. We must **adapt and adopt new learning skills and new ways of teaching and interacting with them**, even if it goes against cultural norms. They process information much quicker.

As institutional leaders, you must:

- **Maintain a Pulse on the Culture:** Have your ear to the ground. Ensure the people you put in these centers understand how to connect with the current generation.
- **Prioritize Interactive Learning:** Implement systems that allow for hands-on interaction, such as giving the kids opportunities to interact with older high school athletes or students involved in extracurricular activities. Make the program as interactive, fun, and valuable as possible, all while ensuring **discipline and structure remain at the core**.
- **Establish Communication Transparency:** Since superintendents and administrators can be removed from the day-to-day ins and outs, it is vital to find a trustworthy person to communicate with regularly. This ensures their vision and goals for the center are actually being acted out, creating **total transparency** across the board.

Fostering Universal Passion

A major responsibility for a superintendent is to figure out a way to pull students into a passionate exchange with some kind of discipline or activity and this must be done on a large scale. I propose implementing a standard that **all children can participate in some form of extracurricular activity**.

While this may sound expensive or impractical, the reality is that the internet and remote opportunities allow us to create:

- Contests
- Drama Clubs
- Art Competitions
- Clubs and group activities

Let's create these spaces via virtual and remote opportunities. Without a passion—something they feel is their own—we are failing to nurture that internal desire in the students.

Partnering for Transformative Change

Partnering with a proven entity like ours—one that has a track record across multiple fields, different backgrounds, and collections of people—takes a huge burden off the district. We have the specific skill set to educate, discipline, train, develop, and mentor, allowing for **greater efficiency** for all parties involved.

It is imperative that we get the right people in the right places doing the right things. The job may seem complicated, but it is not impossible. Through partnerships and collectives, we can put our heads together to staff these centers, in many cases, with the **existing staff that's already in place**. Our role is instrumental in providing the **structure, discipline, and the sustainable infrastructure** needed for long-term success.

We must put egos aside and recognize that the reward of creating something truly transformative far outweighs the possible negativity or fear of the unknown. The same criteria used by a school to select staff are the same criteria we are held to. Repurposing locations and collaborating would be a springboard for **positive publicity, parent and student engagement, and new opportunities** for both students and teachers.

The biggest asset a leader can possess is being **accessible**. When you are accessible to people, it gives them a sense of belonging, and the work becomes more of a group project as opposed to a job or a task. I implore institutional leaders to always keep an open mind and realize that this landscape is ever-changing. We must get ahead of the curve. By implementing programs such as ours, we can hit the reset button on stagnant operations and begin inspiring, empowering, and instilling high character values in these students. The superintendents and principals will be directly responsible for those impactful changes in the lives of those students and their families.

CHAPTER 12

The Logistical Solution: Implementing the Institutional Playbook Onsite

This chapter focuses on the **logistical solution**—the nuts and bolts of taking our proven institutional playbook and implementing it successfully on an individual site, whether you're launching one location or scaling across multiple campuses. From securing the grounds to managing transportation and building strong school partnerships, execution relies on meticulous planning and an unwavering commitment to the children we serve.

Understanding the Magnitude of Our Responsibility

Before we dive into systems and protocols, we must start with the fundamental mindset. I had a mentor who told me, "**Always know your personnel**." When doing this work, you are dealing with people's most prized possession—their children. This is their legacy;

this is whom a lot of people dedicate their every waking moment to.

The responsibility that comes with that is immense. You must always stay **humble** and constantly operate in a mindset of receiving **constructive criticism** and taking feedback. This allows us to continuously fix the system and make it better. Understanding the **magnitude** of working with people's children should always be the front-of- the staff's mind and serving, a top priority.

Groundwork: Preparing the Physical Space

When you are actually implementing these types of programs, **systems and protocols** are number one. Especially when starting off, you're going to want a system that has already been put in place and proven.

Every individual site is going to be unique, depending on the space you're in. I think the biggest initial step is to conduct a **walk-through of the property or the grounds**. You need to see exactly what kind of space you're working with:

- **Indoor and Outdoor Space:** Assess the size and condition of all usable areas.
- **Accessibility and Flow:** Where will you set up the space? Where will equipment go? What spaces are accessible to which age groups? What activities will each specific design zone be used for? How will the kids move through the area?

- **Safety and Restriction:** Where will you restrict movement? What times are designated for snacks?
- **Emergency Planning:** Make a safe plan. In case of fire, which way do you exit? Who is in which group, and who goes with which counselor?

Executing **fire drills** is part of our DCF mandate, but the emphasis I want to place here is that all of this preparation is critical because **it's not important until you need it**. The biggest thing is just to stay ready and prepared.

On the other side of that coin, give yourself some grace. There are going to be some ups and downs and some days where things just don't look perfect. The key is to try to **stick to a script and stick to the plan**. When life forces you to deviate, make sure you:

- **Document properly**.
- Be **transparent** and communicate any changes to the parents so they are not caught off guard.

Solving the Transportation Hurdle

Transportation is often the biggest hurdle in after-school program logistics. Again, it comes back to the understanding that you're moving people's prized possession. **Safety is paramount**, and you must operate with that in mind at all times.

Key Focus Areas for Safe Transport

- **Route Assessment:** Look at the route, the schools you're going to, and what the traffic patterns are like.

- **Driver Mindset:** The driver must not be a person that's in a rush. Being late is bad, but putting people in harm's way is worse. **Don't make something worse by rushing.**
- **Training and Ride-Alongs:** Before a new driver gets on the road, you should always do a drive-along or ride-along, route to route. Train them a time or two to make sure they truly understand the expectations.
- **Vehicle Compliance:** The vehicle must be in compliance. Ensure it has passed inspection and is regularly inspected (at least once a year). Check that all compliance items are up-to-date, including:
  - A fire extinguisher.
  - Water.
  - A first aid kit.
  - A functional **alarm system** that requires the driver to walk to the back of the vehicle to turn it off, preventing any child from being left behind.

The Role of Communication and Preparation

The simple truth is that detours and changes to traffic patterns will happen. When they do, **communication is key**.

I was late one day due to a detour, and the second day, I tried an alternate route that still wasn't working. I had to go into the school and communicate to the front desk, "Listen, this traffic pattern has changed, and there's no way I'm going to be able to get here in the allotted time. Can we work this out until this clears up?" She made the adjustment to keep the kids in the front office. She was aware, not caught off guard, and did not call a parent unnecessarily.

We must also be willing to check ourselves and our usual route. I found a route that saved me five minutes by simply putting it into the GPS, even though I'd been driving the route for two months. **Don't always think you know all the answers**; be willing to run everything through the system as a checks and balance.

Implementation Overcomes the Hurdle

The primary reason implementing our model onsite helps overcome the transportation hurdle is through **preparation, preparation, preparation**.

- We incorporate daily communication between the director and staff about who is being picked up and where they're going.
- We use a system of **checks and balances** to prevent the worst thing that can happen: forgetting a child.
- We have a checklist of required tasks the driver must complete every day—and if they're not done, a corrective action plan is put in place.

Our liability is already high, so we have to do everything we can on the preparation and compliance side to make sure we're in compliance.

Structuring Mutually Beneficial School Partnerships

To build a sustainable program, you need to create strong, **mutually beneficial relationships** with the schools. This is a large part of our secret sauce.

Steps for Effective School Partnership
1. **Formalize the Relationship:** Reach out to the school board or district at the beginning of the year and sign up to become a **licensed business partner**. This elevates our relationship and gives us a certain capacity for interaction.
2. **Tailor Your Approach:** While a general background check is needed just to be on campus, we take it further. We tailor our systems to the schools we are serving and create good working relationships with the staff that help bring the children out.
3. **Offer Resources and Outreach:** We always go to the schools to see if there's any assistance we can offer. This could be:
    - Mentoring kids who are having issues.
    - Donating supplies for activities.
    - Sponsoring events (e.g., providing pizzas or using our A.U. Nutrition brand to sponsor snacks).
4. **Partner with the PTA:** The **Parent-Teacher Association** is a vital part of the school's life. We create partnerships with them, sometimes hosting their meetings or sponsoring their events.

5. **Provide Teacher Appreciation:** We purchase snacks and goodies for the teachers on a designated **Teacher Appreciation Day**. This allows us to connect with the staff, and introduce ourselves.
6. **Creative Marketing:** My director's decision to purchase a popcorn machine—which I questioned at first—is a perfect example. We now sponsor popcorn at school events and use **branded packaging** that includes a QR code introducing parents to our product. This creative close-to-the-community marketing works twofold: it's a partnership tool and an advertising tool.

The bottom line is that partnership works twofold, and we always **reciprocate the energy**. Because we are visible and offer resources, parents call us and say, "I asked about after-school, and the school referred us to you guys."

The Key to Scalability

Scalability for our model is extremely high because we are integrating a proven system into an already existing infrastructure and framework. DCF and similar governing regulations for child interaction exist nationwide.

The fundamental task for scaling is to transition from a motive of passive protection care to developmental, motivational nurturing. We do this by:

- **Staffing for Character:** We create a profile for the necessary character traits for each position and identify the right staff first, based on the day-to-day needs of the campus.
- **The Blueprint:** We provide a **script, a blueprint, a handbook, and a manual of protocols** so staff is not guessing how to handle any situation.
- **Auditing and Accountability:** We go through a process of dress rehearsing and auditing. We assign each staff member a work buddy or an accountability partner so they have someone to check in with.
- **Maintaining an Active Floor:** We operate on an **active floor**, meaning kids are moving around and doing activities. Our ability to maintain continuous success is due to minimizing accidents, which is a result of our strict operational structure and implementation of discipline.

It's hard to scale when you have poor customer service, lack of compliance, lack of transparency, and a lack of structure. The **replicability** of our model depends entirely on maintaining this structure.

Final Logistical Takeaways: Planning and Consistency

Ultimately, logistics is the actual application of the job; it's proving that we can take a concept and consistently maintain and run this system.

The Power of Planning

- **A Schedule is Your Lifeline:** Do not just have curriculums and schedules for compliance reasons—actually use them. They are what save you when things go awry.
- **Contingencies:** When you have a schedule, it's easier to adjust when you need a contingency (e.g., if it's raining and you can't go outside). You can get recalibrated and get back on track.
- **Rehearse the Day:** Write a day down on paper from start to finish and work through it. This will give you an idea of all the tasks needed to complete the job.

Consistency and Safety

- **Harness the Energy:** A firm hand on the scheduling is necessary to control the energy of the room. Once the energy reaches a certain temperature, it takes a while to cool down.
- **Account for Every Second:** Everyone should know what they are doing according to the schedule. We should know where we should be, so we can get back on track if we get off task.
- **"Less is More" with Activity:** We want to be an added value, not a negative influence. If a kid is sick or having a bad day, let them take the activity off. 30 minutes of less is more when it comes to physical activity.

- **Be In Tune:** The staff must be able to identify when a student needs a mental break or an adjustment. This requires a relationship built on trust and communication.
- **No Tolerance Policy:** We have a zero-tolerance policy on certain things, like a child moving around without their group or without permission. A student must say, "Hey, I'm going to the bathroom," so we have an expectation of where they are and a reasonable amount of time for them to return. This is how we prevent a lot of stuff from happening.

In the end, **planning and preparation** are the two foundational takeaways for a successful logistical solution. If we execute the logistics, we prove that we are capable of maintaining the work, which is the largest factor in success when taking on this new challenge.

CHAPTER 13

The Parent-Athlete Dynamic: Nurturing Competition and Passion

This chapter is a call to action, a reflection on one of the most impactful moments in a child's life: the balancing act between a parent's love and a child's intentional pursuit of a passion, be it sports, music, chess, or dance. Without this balance, this interaction, there is no awareness of the child's developmental needs and no true teamwork. My goal is to bring the insights I've gained from working with children daily into your home, shifting the focus to a more micro, in-house solution.

A parent is often the only person who truly wants to see their child become better than them. Accepting and living in that unique position puts everything into perspective. It requires a certain attentiveness, care, and concern—a deep desire for them to be the best version of themselves—that only comes from being around them on a day-to-day basis.

The Groundwork: Intention vs. Impact

I want to start by acknowledging a difficult truth: some of the worst things are done with the best intentions. Many parents, acting on their own experiences and what they thought was right, end up being misguided. When you are too close to a situation, you can't always see it for what it truly is. That's often what happens in the parent-child relationship.

It's a tough job. If you're showing up and putting in the effort as a parent, you've won half the battle. Now, the rest of the battle is about finding people and resources you trust to give you perspective, insight, and options. Parenting is all about adding to a collective think tank to make the best decisions for your child.

Understanding Our Competitive World

It's crucial to understand the environment we live in. America is rooted in competition. Whether you are an athlete or not, you are constantly competing—for resources, opportunity, and attention. Therefore, one of the parent's toughest jobs is to find a way to nurture a child while teaching the fundamentals of competition.

This is where energy often gets misguided. The interaction between parent and child is fundamentally an emotional one. A child doesn't just hear your words; they feel the emotion of what you are feeling. Your words might say, "I'm trying to motivate you," but your energy might say, "I'm frustrated, I'm mad, my expectations have been let down."

We must lay the foundation for parents to understand that our ultimate purpose is to inspire and instill passion, giving children something they can call their own. Our programs are designed to help them start the journey of finding themselves, which is not a process you can capture in a snapshot or a week.

Defining the Dynamic: Teamwork, Devotion, and Confidence

The Parent-Athlete Dynamic (or the Parent-Student-Athlete Dynamic, or simply Parent-Child) is best defined by one word: teamwork. It means coming together to work on a project for the greater good. As I always say, "Sacrifices must be made for the good of the kingdom."

- From the parent's side, it is devotion, love, nurturing, discipline, and responsibility—a responsibility that truly blesses you. It's a self-fulfilling prophecy because when you pour into that child, they will, in turn, pour into you. You receive a great deal of confidence when your children do great things.
- From the child's side, the parent offers an unwavering confidence—the ability to teach someone how to believe, perceive, and accept what to expect. For me and my team, being part of this dynamic is an opportunity to impact growth and

guide lifelong partnerships. It is truly remarkable.

When the Dynamic Breaks Down: Structure vs. Chaos

I've seen this relationship either strengthen or fracture families. The breakdown almost always occurs when there is a lack of discipline, structure, and organization. Children need routine, and when routines and clear expectations are not upheld, communication breaks down.

When communication fails, one side feels the relationship is unfair. For a parent, this can make the relationship feel like a burden or a debt instead of a labor of love.

Frankly, I have to place the primary responsibility on the parents. When a child is born, they are a blank slate. You have the ability to guide and direct that child. While you can't force them into a specific mold, you should be seeking out positive role models and mentors to provide you with good information.

The biggest factors I've seen that cause rifts and fractures are:

- Failure to set the tone for the relationship from the jump.
- A lack of organization, structure, communication, and discipline.
- An absence of clear standards and expectations.

If we do not give children an organized framework to work from, they will create one out of chaos—an unguided, unorganized state that often doesn't meet the expectations of society.

The Power of Setting the Tone

When things go well, it is a beautiful sight. The parents or guardians set the tone, the structure is in place, and they leverage resources, understanding the truth of the old African proverb: "It takes a village to raise a child."

I've been blessed to have a bird's-eye view of countless parent-child relationships, which has made me a better father. It has given me the ability to step back out of my own expectations and realize I am raising a separate, sentient being who must learn to maneuver through life on their own. Our relationship will mature as they mature, so we must be raising them with a mindset of preparing them for maturity, not raising them as if they will always be children.

This takes a page from the movie Inception: the idea is to infuse the good in our children, but the key is they must think it was their own idea.

Coaching the Parent: From Competitor to Supporter

Many parents are, consciously or unconsciously, reliving their own dreams through their children. We have to inspire parents to see that their role is to be the cameras—the lens, the good guy.

In our program, we insert ourselves as the "bad guy" or the disciplinarian who handles accountability and performance expectations. The parents' job is simply to reinforce our message and document the child's:

- Energy
- Effort
- Hustle
- Passion
- Focus

Parents should not set performance expectations. They should inspire and motivate the work ethic, passion, and core beliefs. Trainers and coaches are the ones who should be discussing performance. Think of it like a business: the investors (parents) don't work directly with the factory workers (the child's performance); there is a professional middleman (the coach/trainer) to handle the pressure.

As a parent of an athlete, you must understand that there is nothing in the moment of a competition that can be done to change the outcome. Either you prepared for it, or you did not. Therefore, the only appropriate expectations for a parent to set are based on preparation—the amount of energy, effort, and passion put in beforehand.

It's easy to take pride in our children's accomplishments, but it is not your job to make your child feel pride or sadness based on their performance in a game. The purpose of the activity is for them to find something they love, learn, and gain life experience from. Your new experience is being a parent, which involves guiding someone else's Energy, Effort, Hustle, Passion, and Focus.

You have to transition from competing to supporting competition.

If you have a problem communicating with your child during a game, you must remove yourself from close proximity. I sometimes make parents sit in the outfield because they cannot stop themselves from trying to intervene. You do not have the ability to publicly embarrass your child or put unrealistic expectations on them.

Your child has the right to fail because without failure, there is no learning, and there is no development.

Practical Steps for Supportive Parenting

The biggest actionable steps parents can take revolve around scheduling and organization. We have to communicate why we are doing things. With kids today processing so much data, we must be able to explain our reasoning, but once we say something, we must do it. Follow-through is of the utmost importance.

5 Actionable Steps for Parents

1. Set and Lead the Schedule: Get up early and timely. Your job is to provide more than food; it's to provide social and spiritual stimulation, love, and structure. Prepare things for your child

before they wake, and always wake them with a loving spirit. My own frustration over being behind the eight ball led to me being aggressive—I realized it wasn't their frustration, it was mine.

2. Use Pre-Explained Consequences: Don't discuss consequences when you are angry. The consequence should already be a fixed law, calmly and firmly applied. The consequence is the consequence. If you struggle with firmness, put it on paper (house rules/law) and stick to it. This gives the child crucial boundaries and parameters.

3. Prioritize Personal Development Before Reward: Before any free activity or reward, the child must complete a personal development activity—reading, writing, working on spelling, or practicing for their chosen extracurricular.

4. Set Participation Guidelines: If you are the financier of an activity, you have the right to set the terms of the agreement. This means setting participation guidelines—a set amount of time devoted to skill development. If a job demanded more energy and effort, we would have a conference. We must become more business-oriented and teach them that effort matters. This is the core principle of our Business of Me course, which teaches life skills and focuses on getting kids passionate and focused so they don't drift.

5. Master Tone and Timing: Never discuss things when you are angry. You have the right to step

back. Remember this profound truth: It is the responsibility of the person giving the message for the message to be received properly. A child often freezes up when a parent's energy is improper, preventing them from hearing the message. Tone and timing are everything.

The Prep-to-Performance Standard

For parents of athletes, a non-negotiable standard must be set: Any conversation with a child about performance must first be set with a standard of energy and effort put toward the preparation of that activity.

If we are not going to question their Energy, Effort, Hustle, Passion, and Focus before the game, we do not have the moral high ground to question their productivity or production after the game.

If those standards are in place, and you need to question an outcome, it is always posed better as a question over ice cream than a cynical comment after a disappointment. You must also allow the coaches to handle the competitive environment. When you question your child's energy during a game, disrespect is likely, because they are often trying their absolute best, and your interruption is a violation of their safe space to compete.

Final Wisdom: The Steward, the Shepherd, and the Goal

As a parent, your role is to be a steward and a shepherd—a guiding light, not the light itself. Your role is to experience life with your child, to be a record keeper of who they are.

Sometimes, we lose the opportunity to have truly meaningful friendships with our children because we are too focused on parenting them. But if we don't parent them with the right amount of discipline and structure early on, we will not be able to enjoy those beautiful moments with them later.

The overall end goal is to inspire and empower your child to be a sound decision-maker who can matriculate through life on their own core beliefs. Your role is to be a supporting resource and to find other supporting resources.

Give Yourself Grace

Don't be too hard on yourself. We all make mistakes, and children have a short memory—they will forgive you. Never get to a point where you feel you can't apologize to your child. You must lead by example because they will not exhibit any positive behavior they are not taught.

If your relationship with your child feels one-sided, it signals a lack of communication. Make sure you have regular, non-business-oriented communication—just talking about life—to get a true baseline for who they are. This way, when something goes awry, you can identify the problem early and combat it with a corrective action plan.

Set Standards and Teach Etiquette

- Don't reward bad behavior. If your child is not complying with the expectations, do not reward the lack of effort. Rewarding bad behavior teaches them that your word means nothing.
- Prepare them for the world. The world will interact with your child much differently than you do. Do not enable them to be victims.
- Lead the whole person, not just the athlete. Teach your child etiquette and how to interact. Always have them thank their coaches and trainers for their time and effort.
- Be coachable yourself. Respect the coaches' leadership. As I always say, "You don't gotta like it, but you gotta respect it." If your child desires to be a leader, they must first learn to follow, as that's the only way to receive instruction.
- Be attentive and focused in team settings. In a team environment, your child's behavior should not be an outlier; they should be complying with the group and taking in the instruction. The private setting is when they can separate themselves.

Your child is there to develop a skillset and a passion—a vehicle that will hopefully take them as far as they want to go in life. Be appreciative of the opportunity and teach your child to be the same.

CHAPTER 14

The In-House Playbook: Bringing the Micro Solution Home

This chapter is about taking the core principles—the structure, discipline, and intentionality—that we use in our facility and adapting them for the home and parenting space. If our model works daily with dozens of kids, its fundamental concepts can certainly be adopted to bring order and positive development into your family environment. When we talk about "bringing the program home," we're talking about how parents can model and execute those same principles in their own house.

Structure, Scheduling, and the Law of the Land

With us, everything is going to revolve around structure and scheduling. If you have children and don't have a schedule, you are living in chaos. You just have to accept that reality. Time is always short when children are around because they don't stop moving, needing, or consuming. What we have to do is organize the consumption.

This commitment to calendaring and scheduling is not just for kids; it's an essential tool for personal growth in general. I've recently come to the conclusion that I need to do it consistently, holding myself accountable to scheduling everything.

The first thing we must do is create a schedule. Just like the kids at our after-school programs or satellite locations—every child has a specific set of activities to do at a set time.

- Establish a Daily Flow: When they arrive, they put their book bags up at a specific time, get a snack at this time, do baseball at this time, basketball at this time, clean up at this time, and go home at this time.
- Create Calmness and Expectation: This consistent, ritualistic routine creates a sense of normalcy, calmness, and expectation. We can now anticipate outcomes and predict behavior because we're doing it on a consistent basis. Scheduling is the number one thing.

Secondly, you must set the rules and guidelines in place. We go over the rules formally on day one with new kids. A child is always coming from another environment, so they need to be affirmed on the rules of the house—the "law of the land." This ensures the expectations are known. If they make a mistake or "slide," they already understand what the consequence is.

The Power of Follow-Through and Recalibrating Leverage

The third and most crucial point is the follow-through. You must follow through with what you say.

If I tell a student, "If you don't stop doing what you're doing, you're not going to get a snack for a week," they are not getting a snack for a week. I might cut it down to three days, but I am not going to turn around the next day and give them a snack. If you say, "There's no bounce house today" because of bad behavior, you don't roll out the bounce house.

If you don't follow through, the kids don't think you mean business; they don't think you're serious. If they don't believe what you say, they're not going to do it. At home, this means if you say, "If you don't clean this room up by a set time, you're not getting dessert," you have to stick to that. It's not about you, the parent; it's the rule, it's the law. The rules are in place so we all have a safe space to interact and grow. Without rules, there is chaos.

Mastering the Transactional Interaction

Kids learn to manipulate parents against each other, and they also try to bully you with chaos—acting out because they know you won't apply physical punishment (which we don't do at the facility, so we hold that to be true). They gain leverage by thinking, "All I have to do is scream and cry and get my way."

The reality is, in my home and in the facility, I have veto power. I'm the president. I don't micromanage every detail, but at the moment I don't like something, I have the ability to restrict any movement or activity because I control all movement and activity. The moment they understand that, they comply.

You need to recalibrate the leverage. It's not acting like a tyrant—I took my daughter to a pool party—but I will not let her manipulate me. When you say something, that's it. My own mother would tell me a rule one time, and even if it didn't come up again for two years, the rule was still the rule. We have to prepare our children for the world they enter daily. Stop looking at it only from the perspective of someone you love who you don't want to see have discomfort. Sometimes, I tell the kids "no" just because, so they don't think that just because they're not asking for a lot means they can always have their way.

Cultivating Desire and Managing Screen Time

A big problem we see in the home is the kid who is not necessarily "bad" but is not motivated. That lack of motivation often comes from a lack of exposure, a lack of expectation, and a lack of identifying a passion or skill. If they're not active and trying different things, the only desire they develop is for the things they consume, like electronics.

A child who goes home and just watches TV and does nothing cannot be expected to be a high achiever in school. Success is often tied to effort. If the effort isn't there, you can't have any predictable or anticipated outcome. As much as anything, we should have expectations for our children.

For example, at our house, we don't look at tablets for longer than 30 minutes at a time. After those 30 minutes, the clock resets, and we have to go do some kind of personal development or growth activity. This could be arts and crafts, or going outside to play. The goal is to avoid them sitting in the house watching tablets all day, because no matter how long you allow it, it's never enough. The parent then feels ungratefulness, but the reality is the activity was probably never meant to be done that way.

These concepts may not make parents feel good in the initial moment, but they are meant to inspire a certain amount of responsibility and awareness of that responsibility, and to empower the parent to realize: "You can."

An Illustrative Story: Holding the Line

I was at my daughter's friend's pool party. When it was time to go, my daughter started the whole "I don't want to go" scenario. After the initial finesse, I stopped, got down in front of her, and looked her in the eyes. I said, "Rain, it's time to go. Daddy has to leave. If I sacrifice and brought you to the party, you have to be able to understand it's time to go. If not, the next time I just won't bring you."

I gave her five minutes to collect her things, or we'd start taking away privileges. She complied. One of the fathers there was completely in awe. "She's just going to do what you say?" he asked. My answer was simple: "Yeah. What is she going to do, not do what I say? I drove, I paid. I'm him. She has to do what I say."

The issue for many parents is a lack of follow-through. When a child screams, they are trying to bully you with chaos. You have to realize that they can only fuss and scream for so long. At some point, they are going to have to come to terms with the fact that you are not giving in.

Implementing Discipline Without Being Overbearing

The secret to applying discipline and structure without becoming overbearing is to remove the personal emotion from the interaction; make it transactional.

- Use Transactional Communication: If your child is old enough, send them a text or a related message: "Hey, I need you to clean your room up by this time. We have someone coming over."
- Maintain Tone Control: Try not to raise your voice when it's not necessary. Raise your voice

only when you need immediate attention. Once you have their attention, there's no need to continue to elevate your tone.
- Identify Controllable Desires: Identify the activities or items you control that they want, and restrict them when they are not in compliance. At the facility, we institute programs that the kids enjoy so the parents have something to restrict if the child isn't responding properly. This helps you get the balance of leverage back in your favor.
- Use Active Consequences: Instead of "I'm sorry," which puts no pressure on the bad decision, use consequences that require effort. For me, I'm big on push-ups, sit-ups, or running. You have to make the uncomfortable thing normal, because in life, they've got to learn the skill of doing things they don't want to do.

It is absolutely important for parents and guardians to understand that in a behavioral sense, it is "us versus them." Your children have a goal and a motive, just as you do, and they will team up. Parents must stay on the same path and the same page.

You don't have to be aggressive to discipline, but assertiveness is key. Understand that you are asking them to do something for their benefit. Our job as parents is to teach life skills—to teach them how to manage life. Discipline is a prerequisite for raising a healthy, balanced, well-adjusted child.

The "Line Theory"

If they lack discipline, they're going to intrude on someone else's personal space and boundaries. I call this the "Line Theory." In all relationships, invisible lines exist. When someone intrudes on your space—pushing past the line—they erase the old line and create a new one. It's your responsibility to re-correct and re-address that line. When we fail to teach kids discipline, we don't teach them that other people have boundaries. This leads to them intruding on others, alienation, a bad reputation, and a downward spiral. We want to ensure they are respected, well-mannered, and well-received.

Small Daily Habits for Culture Change

Small, daily habits are what change a household's culture. We try to mimic the things we do here:

- Everything Has a Place: When kids get home, have them immediately take off their shoes and put them in a bin. Everything has a place and a purpose. Make them accountable at all times. Don't let them run free all evening and then make them clean up right before bed. It's not practical. The best way is to "stay ready" by staying tidy.
- Teach Self-Policing: We teach our students to police themselves. If every book bag is supposed to be on a hook, and one is not, everyone has to run. This applies a concept of "one bad apple spoils the bunch" and teaches them to self-correct. If

we're not teaching them to police themselves, we will always have to police them. The policing should be an internal audit.
- Respectful Communication: Kids don't talk while adults are talking. If I'm talking, they have to wait, say "Excuse me," and stand there until I acknowledge them. You cannot allow a child to just burst into a conversation. If they do, you must correct the behavior, because if you don't, you are accepting it.
- Principle Over Convenience: I made my son pick up the socks he left on the stairs, even though I walked past them four times. Could I have done it? Yes, but it was a matter of principle. I was teaching him cleanliness, not teaching myself cleanliness.

We teach through struggle—active, controlled struggle. We put them up against challenges, see how they respond, and talk them through it.

The Transformation of James

We had a kid named James, a good athlete, but his mom was carrying his book bag and equipment bag when he came in for his first session. I immediately told her to put it down. I looked at him and said, "Bro, that's your bag. She paid for it, you carry it." It was about setting the tone and helping him understand: "That's your mom, that's a woman. Why would you want her to carry your bag?"

James wasn't a bad kid; he was just enabled to intrude on his parents' personal space because they didn't have boundaries. I had to correct him repeatedly for talking while his mom and I were speaking.

After about a month, I noticed he was carrying his own bag, and he wasn't asking his mom to find his stuff. I asked his mom about it, and she said he was being much more mature and helpful. She realized that I had made him aware of the things he was not doing. He started to adopt a better mindset. She even began referring back to me: "What would Coach JP say about this?" That shift of awareness, adopted by both parent and child, transformed their interactions.

The Vision for the Home

Home is a safe space, a sanctuary. Everyone should have the opportunity to express themselves in a safe, respectful manner. But parents have to have boundaries, and kids should have bedtimes and actionable activities. They should be managing basic tasks on their own, like putting clothes in the bin or tidying their room.

If you have lost control, it's okay—it doesn't make you a bad parent. But you cannot allow the child to continue on a path that won't serve them in life. The biggest thing is that they must identify right from wrong and understand consequences so they can correct their own behavior. If we have to walk around and correct them every single day for the same things, they're not really learning or growing.

Ultimately, you have to have an overall picture or vision of where you want your house to be.

- What is the vision for what your home looks like from 6:30 to 9:00 p.m.?
- What is the desired flow?
- How do you want their time spent in a perfect world?

If you have never sat down and thought about that, it's going to be hard to create it. You must go through and organize the actual time slots, like you're scheduling them. If you do that, you'll see a tremendous impact on the interaction with your child and their overall output.

Kids crave structure. A lot of times, the things we think they "just gotta have"—like tablets—are quickly forgotten if we shift their focus with an activity. We have to separate our fear of our children being uncomfortable so we can properly guide and rear them.

Don't allow the weight of responsibility to cripple you or render you powerless. You have power, you have control, you have a say. Just because they don't like what you say doesn't make you mean. Don't allow them to bully you with words or play on your emotions. You're the captain of the boat. You know the instruments, the time frame, and the expectation. The only thing that matters is getting them to their destination on time, healthy, happy, and safe.

CHAPTER 15

Mentoring the Child, Not Just the Jit

Chapter 15 is about mentoring the child, not just the jit. As we step into this discussion, we must first remember a foundational truth about the people we guide: we all exist with dual personalities, dual existences.

The Dual Existence: Avatar and Spirit

Your child is who you know them to be—their physical avatar—the person becoming in front of you. But inside that body exists a spirit being. We accept the fact that there is a larger, spiritual part of us connected to something greater. The biggest thing that has to be remembered is that the being that entered into your care could be older than you as the parent. We simply don't know if they are young or old in spirit.

I want to preface this with that thought to lay the foundation for how much reverence, responsibility, and respect we should give to that person or that being we interact with every day. That being is very similar to you; you are alike in many respects. They chose to give you the opportunity to steward them—to be influenced by them and for you to influence them. That is a tremendous responsibility.

At Athlete University, we approach every kid, child, athlete, and student with this perspective.

Mentoring the Child vs. Mentoring the Jit

To understand the difference between mentoring the child and mentoring the "jit," we must first define what a jit is. "Jit" is a layman's term for a kid, representing the immature side of a child. The phrase "jitbug" used to be common—a dancing, moving, rambunctious, and overly active kind of person. It was a character, almost like an avatar. We refer to kids as jits when they are exemplifying the characteristics and behaviors we exhibited as children.

There is the jit personality and the polished child personality—the person we aspire for them to be. 9 times out of 10, there is a battle between who will be the dominant personality in the present moment.

The Key Distinction

Personality	Focus & Mindset	Mentorship Approach
The Jit	Base wants and needs, instant gratification, burning the candle at both ends, lack of awareness of their impact.	Speak in terms they can relate to, find commonality, and make comparisons to relatable life lessons or role models.
The Child	Has accepted discipline and structure as a way of life, is operating within an infrastructure, and trusts the process.	Institute and implement more structure in your tone, verbiage, and body language. Firm, but focused on maximizing their growth.

The difference in mentoring is understanding the mindset of each and meeting them on their level. When mentoring a jit, I am stretching their capacity to reach an elevated state. The goal is how do we get the jit to grow? The jit will grow through identifying with them and then creating a comparison to a life lesson or someone they look up to.

A child is more structured and in compliance. You receive less resistance when asking them to do things outside their comfort zone. A jit resists anything uncomfortable; a child trusts that it is for their betterment and growth.

Balancing Mentorship, Accountability, and Empathy

To effectively guide a young person, we must balance these three cornerstones.

- Empathy: This is the basis of everything we do. We must understand that we were all jits at one point, and in that state, we needed grace, temperance, tolerance, and forgiveness. We empathize and sympathize, but this does not mean we give in. Empathy means we are emotionally sympathetic and won't hold their current behavior against them. We show empathy by giving second chances and having open communication—by not throwing them away.
- Mentorship: This is the process itself. Empathy is a component encompassed within the mentorship process. The responsibility to mentor comes from the feeling that we can help—that there is value we can add. When you become a mentor, you now understand there is an end goal, a

journey to be completed. Mentorship is the job, the duty, the service.
- Accountability: This is also encompassed in mentorship. We hold them accountable because we want to see them grow, develop, and reach the finish line. Because we are mentors, we must maintain our standards, and the accountability structure ensures they continue to put in the energy, effort, hustle, passion, and focus that is mandatory for growth.

Case Study: From Eight-Year-Old Jit to D-I Prospect

My experience with "Edward" is a perfect example of this long-term approach. 10 years ago, Edward came to me as an 8-year-old. He was green, big but inexperienced, and it became clear he needed much more than just baseball training. He was a jit—and not only a jit, but a rich jit, which brought an element of entitlement.

I was ready to step away because he was not coachable yet, but his father pulled me aside. He saw the struggle and acknowledged his own absence. He asked me to help them on the journey and make it a long-term commitment. In that moment, I felt conflicted, but it became the basis for the philosophy we use today.

The father would often express frustration, but I always told him, "He's playing with house money. This is the worst he'll ever be. The only thing we have to do is not let him quit." None of the small struggles matter if they're not doing it at 18. The goal is maintaining momentum and preventing the stopping and starting that derails progress.

- 11-12 Years Old: The light bulb came on. He began to mature, perform at a high level, and interact more with others.
- The Litmus Test: When he was 15, he started on the varsity team as a freshman at a high school. This was a critical test that showed the work had given him the necessary notoriety and opportunity.
- Learning the Hard Lessons: Going into his junior year, he made a pivotal decision to switch high schools. This proved difficult—he wasn't playing. He learned the hard lesson: "Don't put yourself in a position that you don't control the narrative." After all that work, you have to control it.
- Finding the Path: He transitioned to a homeschool program, is now a senior, a high-level performer, and is receiving attention from colleges and scouts. Worst-case scenario, he will be a Division I baseball player; best-case, he'll be drafted.

Watching him drive himself to the facility one day, without his parents, was a priceless moment. It hit me: "Wow, he's really here now." This story, and others like it, defined my purpose and showed me the ability to take a long-term approach to development.

Defining Long-Term Success

At the Elite University, we gauge success a little differently. Our idea of long-term success is the student-athlete meeting their goals. This is their journey. We focus on helping them identify their goals so that their participation is intentional, not just going along with the flow.

We consider our program successful when we check in with them and they are well-adjusted, well-rounded, balanced, and productive members of society. Our purpose is to empower them to show they can do anything they choose. Success, for us, is them continuing to move through life at their pace and in their intended direction.

The Parent's Multifaceted Role

Parents and mentors need to understand the fundamental responsibilities of guidance.

The biggest thing to remember is to always keep the long-term goal in mind, but don't get fixed on the end result. The path will not be a straight line. They will make different decisions, and success looks different for different people.

When mentoring, you are wearing multiple hats:
- Brother/Sister
- Father/Mother
- Provider
- Spiritual Leader
- Friend

- Disciplinarian

You have to be able to move in and out of all of these capacities at different times. Keep a perspective on where the kid is and the environment they are experiencing.

Guiding Principles for Mentors
- Prioritize Listening: Let them talk so you can figure out what they don't know. Once you realize what is missing, you can redirect their mindset and get them recalibrated.
- Be Present: You must have a real relationship with anyone you mentor and be in tune and alive with the kid.
- Respect Their Clock: Everybody has their own biological clock, their own timetable for growth. Continue to put the work in.
- Model the Work: The work we do as mentors is even more important than the work we ask of them. They are learning how to work, how to engage, and how to have patience from us. We must be mindful at all times of our audience and our responsibility.

A Final Charge to Jits and Children
To the jits: Realize it's a big world out there, and the best thing you can do is find somebody you can trust. One of the most important decisions you will ever make in life is who you choose to accept information

from. When you are around people who care, don't worry about whether you like what they tell you or not—just continue to listen so they will continue to pour into you.

To the child: Just keep going. Stay on the path. Never hold yourself too high, never hold yourself too low. Always be positive and ask questions. Your biggest asset is having access to resources and being able to bounce ideas off of them so you can make better decisions. And finally, practice active decision-making. You only get good at making decisions by making them, but you have to prove you are making good decisions so the adults in your life will continue to give you the opportunity to make them.

Conclusion

This final chapter is where we transition from the system to the soul. We have systematically laid out the architecture of our holistic development model—from the 3:00 to 6:00 p.m. battlefield to the quantifiable return on investment (ROI) and the playbooks for institutions and families. Now, as we close, it's essential to step back and re-anchor our efforts in the fundamental truth: we are engaging with beings. This perspective is the ultimate driver of the mission, the movement, and the enduring impact we seek to create.

The Ripple Effect: Beyond Data and Dollars

It is easy, especially in today's world, to lose sight of the core purpose. We start looking at stats, numbers, and trackable data, and in doing so, we sometimes lose track of the human element. The measurable results—the enhanced engagement, the academic improvement, the scholarships—are vital. They are the proof that the model works. But they are not the reason we do the work.

We have to understand that every thought, word, and action has a ripple effect of immense proportion. Your presence has the ability to impact another being, who will in turn go and impact other beings. When you operate with this understanding, you recognize the gravity of your role.

We must always keep in the front of our minds that we are all here to nurture and steward with one another. Our ultimate goal is for love to conquer all, and for us to promote and uplift everyone. As one person once profoundly stated, "We all look different on the outside, but on the inside, everybody's the same."

This viewpoint means we should not choose who we engage with based on outward appearance. If you are truly trying to help someone, you must:

- Monitor them: Observe their behavior and patterns.
- Study them: Understand their individual needs, strengths, and challenges.
- Engage them: Meet them where they are.

This philosophy dictates that your primary focus is them, not you.

From Apprenticeship to Self-Fulfilling Prophecy

For me, the system we built didn't start with a price tag or a business plan; it started with the work. Before I ever charged a dollar for my services or built this into the packageable, sellable product it is today, I was on the field. I was active in kids' lives, doing the work across different states and places. I built the skill set. I learned. I did my apprenticeship.

This foundational work is crucial because when the foundation is set and rooted in purpose and alignment, what you are doing becomes a self-fulfilling prophecy. The true beauty of this journey is being able to watch other people move, grow, act, and achieve inside of something that started as a concept for you, which you then manifested and embodied. It is truly a transcendent experience.

This entire process — writing this book and going through this therapeutic exercise of laying out the structure — has helped me identify some dormant passions and solidify my purpose. We are just getting started, and there are many more offerings to come.

Embracing Uncomfortability for Growth

I want the readers to understand that the tone of this book is not meant to be incriminating, personal, or antagonizing. I am simply passionate about everything I do and say, and I stand on what I've articulated. If this book has rubbed you the wrong way, perhaps that discomfort was needed.

As a baseball player at heart, I live by one truth that I tell all my athletes, regardless of their sport: In order to be great, you have to learn to become comfortable being uncomfortable. We only grow when we step outside of what is easy or familiar.

Therefore, I urge every reader to:

- Embrace discomfort.
- Embrace change.
- Create structure and schedule.
- Put discipline and love at the forefront of everything you do.

And finally, I must acknowledge the inspiration behind this mission. While we separate systems and beliefs, the reality is that something is guiding everything, and it serves us all to acknowledge that higher purpose.

Thank you to all who have read this book. I hope you enjoyed the journey and that you will now take these playbooks and principles and apply them to your own life, family, and organization. The journey to unlocking a child's full potential is not over; it is just beginning.

THE 3-TO-6 PM BLUEPRINT

CONSULTING
- Families
- Institutions
- Municipalities

CORPORATE WORKSHOPS/ SPEAKING
- Community Engagement Initiatives
- Corporate Team-Building Workshops
- Sports Industry Topics

ATHLETIC DEVELOPMENT
- After and Before School Programs
- Sports Training and Camps

MENTORSHIP
- After-School Mentorship Programs
- Athlete Mentorship Programs
- Parent-Athlete Dynamic Workshops

PERSONAL DEVELOPMENT
- In-House Personal Playbook Development
- Micro Solution Implementation

CONTACT & CONNECT
 BUSINESS PHONE: (321) 234-7873
 EMAIL: Puremomentum36@gmail.com
 WEBSITE: www.Puremomentumsports.com
 INSTAGRAM @Pure_Momentum_AU
 FACEBOOK: @Pure Momentum, LLC

www.ingramcontent.com/pod-product-compliance
Lightning Source LLC
Chambersburg PA
CBHW022109090426
42743CB00008B/778